Spaghetti for Breakfast

A Parent Handbook
for Remembering What You Know

by
Carolyn Harden

Azalea Art Press
Sonoma · California

ISBN: 978-1-943471-91-1

Cover Photo
by Jay Harden

Dedication

To Camilla and Ben,
the children we always wanted,
who like to dream.

CONTENTS

**Chapter 2:
Building Self-Esteem**

Chapter 3
Kid Power

Chapter 4
When Problems Arise, Improvise!

Chapter 5:
How Is The Climate?

Preface by Jay Harden

What can I, the editor of my wife's life work, say here about her? First and foremost she was the greatest thing that ever happened to me, the greatest love of my life for as long as she was here, 42 years — and I knew her for 28 of those.

When I met her in the fall of 1958, I didn't notice I had been struck by lightning. Her dazzling smile, her soft charm, her natural happiness, her exuberant enthusiasm, intoxicated me then and ever after. And I could make her laugh!

We dated off and on and dated others until that day sitting together on a stone wall looking over a mountain valley. I was 15 and she was 14. There we decided what we were going to do with the rest of our lives. Her passion was to be a teacher. My passion was to fly. And we discovered our passions were compatible and promised we would support each other's.

We were innocent enough and strong enough and in love enough to decide on that day, May 8, 1959, that we would marry as soon as we could, as soon as one of us graduated from college. We knew that would be eight years later. We never dated another and married the day after college graduation.

I can say this about Carolyn with all the certainty my heart holds: she died without an enemy in the world. Everyone eventually surrendered to her silent invitation to become a friend and unconsciously gravitated to her.

Our daughter says I put her on a pedestal. Fair enough, though I disagree. My wife was a human being with flaws. There were other things too minor to mention. I smiled at her idiosyncrasies, like the way she unconsciously rubbed her nose horizontally, above her lips, when it itched.

I asked her once, "When we first met, what about me attracted you?" She said she fell in love with my eyelashes!

She was an only child and still very dependent on her mother when we married. She cried as we drove from Georgia, from the only town she ever knew, to live in California for three years. There she flowered into a Fully Functioning Human Being, an FFHB. And she cried again when we had to leave our home and friends there for New England. And she kept growing. And I grew with her. I wanted to keep up. She supported my career and dreams as I did for her. Teaching was the joy in her soul, her dream, and her destiny. She was a teacher everywhere we lived. It was my joy to help her follow her passion.

I can go on, and I will in my published memoirs. You get the picture, and the picture was Carolyn, a beauty from the inside to out.

Introduction by Carolyn Harden

The Purpose of This Book

Parents need inspiration. Inspiration is hope and hope is the intention of this book. I have taught the contents of this book to thousands of parents in hundreds of courses over the years with proven success.

We all want our children to be successful. Yet, a significant gap exists between what we *know* about child development and what we *do* to help our children achieve success.

This book is intended as a map to help you close this gap. Like a map, this book will provide direction and will help you remember what you already know. But, also like a map, it will not specify which route you must take or how long you should stay.

This is a practical handbook on the human side of parenting. It is intended to help parents raise a Fully Functioning Human Being, or FFHB, as described by Carl Rogers.

This book is not hard to do. It is continually encouraging. It is a practical book, not a technical one with overwhelming information that requires processing to be useful.

Don't let the information paralyze or scare you. Let it guide you in your parenting decisions. In turn, you will learn to be an enthusiastic and motivating guide for your children as they embark on the remarkable trip called learning.

Although the focus of this book is on solving parenting problems, it is also a book about human growth and development, regardless of age. Nurturing the human spirit in all its creative wonder is a soul-satisfying lifetime experience for those who brave the challenge.

This book is written from experience and accurate information. In each chapter you will, no doubt, find something useful, or something that you vaguely knew that will lead you to a specific strategy right now in your own family.

Developing Autonomy

Parents today need more self-confidence. This book is intended to raise your self-confidence and competence. It will help you develop autonomy in yourself and your child.

Remember that our parents weren't perfect; we aren't perfect parents; and our children won't be perfect parents; and that's all OK.

This book answers four questions. What is autonomy? How important is it? Who wants it? How can parents and teachers develop it in children? This book is for parents and teachers to help children develop autonomy.

Autonomy is the thing most desired by all people, yet for some parents, autonomy of their child is the most feared. Remember that our children are in their apprenticeship with us for their own autonomous parenthood to come. Also be aware that our child is often a magnet drawing our parenting into their own immaturity.

The home and the school cannot develop autonomy alone. They must work together. The underlying concepts here clarify both roles and build mutual confidence to work together for a child's success.

Information in this book will provide a natural communication vehicle between a parent and a teacher on behalf of a child. The underlying concepts clarify parent and teacher roles and build mutual confidence, so that both work cooperatively together for a child's success.

This book may also be useful for elementary and secondary teachers who want to understand the relationship between autonomy and education and want to explain to parents how their classroom activities promote autonomy.

Who Can Benefit From This book

I have known many bewildered parents without the educational background they wish they had, who tell me, "I will do everything I can to help my kid because my kid is important. If I can help, I will be able to relieve my mind of guilt. I want to learn things I can do to help my child." These parents also want to foster self-esteem, creativity, and curiosity in their child.

There is a lot of stress at home and school today. This book helps relieve much of that stress and frees up more energy to be productive parents. This book will relieve the bewildered parent's mind, allow them to do something specific to help their child, and better understand the purpose of activities in the classroom.

This book is:

To remind parents and teachers of their feelings and experiences forgotten or ignored. Once remembered and under-

stood, they help teach a parent and teacher to naturally use what they know, feel their autonomy, and then develop it in children.

To connect readers with what they already know, wherever they are in their growth, and help them continue on with the development of their individual lives.

For parents who want their children to feel better about themselves than they did, to be better problem solvers than they were, to be more independent as a child than they were, and to keep the sense of wonder that they misplaced.

In addition, this book will be useful as a text for college instructors, and as a resource for daycare providers, parent educators, school counselors and childcare center directors who can recommend this book to parents and say, "This is why we are doing what we are doing in school. This is something you can use yourself so we can work as a team toward a common goal for your child."

The reader will benefit from this book by being a better observer of children in and out of school and will better understand the value of self-esteem at home and school to help children feel better about themselves.

How to Use This Book

Just a brief mention of what you won't find in this book. You won't find anything new. Basically, parenting is hard work and there are no recipes and no simple answers. But this handbook will help you remember what you already know about parenting.

This book is a distillation of core universal parenting principles. It is deceptive in both its length and simplicity. Using this book *does not* require you to master any new technical skills or educational theory. It *does* require committed action on your part based on a new understanding of what you may have forgotten about kids. It also assumes you really want to help your child to the point of examining and possibly changing your own behavior.

If you learn just one thing from this book, learn how to change and influence behavior (yours and your child's) so both of you will feel good about your parenting. If you can adapt and apply these principles as little as 10% of the time, you'll be one step closer to closing the gap between what you know about raising kids and what you can do to help them.

Here is your homework assignment before reading this book:

Decide on five things I want to teach my child before he or she is 18.

Think about what am I doing now to make this happen?

I hope you will enjoy reading this book cover to cover. Then again, you may benefit simply by checking chapter titles and reading just the parts which seem interesting or momentarily relevant.

As with most handbooks, you can keep this book on a shelf and use it when problems arise. You will get the best results by absorbing the parts that will help you get through the "everydays" of your own personal life.

Spaghetti for Breakfast

A Parent Handbook
for Remembering What You Know

CHAPTER 1:
ON BEING AND RAISING AN ADULT

Being an Adult

We all want to guide our children to become independent adults and feel good about themselves. Unfortunately, you can't teach your child to be an adult if you don't recognize and understand what you do and do not know about adult behavior. You must be an adult in order to raise an adult. An adolescent can't raise an adult.

Many people, including Daniel Webster, define an adult as simply a "grown-up." We know being an adult is, of course, more, much more. An adult has a good sense of self. An adult is in charge of his own emotions and takes full responsibility for his own life. Self-responsibility is not only the key to being an adult, it is also the hallmark of self-esteem.

Children observe and copy how we adults build ourselves up and tear ourselves down. You will find your success as a parent and the future success of your child will greatly depend on a keen understanding of this vague intangible called self-esteem.

Begin by considering your own self-esteem and patterns of behavior. Are you in charge of your emotions? Are you a fully functioning, self-sufficient, and responsible adult? Understanding yourself is a necessary prerequisite to effectively lead your children to independence and a strong sense of self. Understanding yourself is the hard work of parenting.

We will talk more about building your child's self-esteem later. The point here is that you must examine your own self-esteem and put your own house in order, so to speak, before you can effectively guide your children to a strong sense of self.

Historic Parenting

Parenting used to be the sole responsibility of the mother. The father was the source of economic security, but the mother was the final decision maker on most family things and in the more frequent, seemingly minor things.

But times have changed and, to no one's surprise, the world has gotten more complicated. Parenting has finally emerged as an important subject for learning, a recognized team effort, and a shared joy.

Parenting is the broadest of family functions, the management system, the glue, if you will, that holds the family together in the face of constant change. But good parenting is not a technical specialty limited to the talented few. Parents know more than they think they do.

Parenting closes the gap between what we know and what we do. The roots of parenting are in all of us who love and care for children. Learning is change, and growth is knowing, doing, and understanding.

The big dilemma for today's parents is a lack of confidence in what they do. There is no shortage of advice. But this book is different in that it asks you to remember what you already know about good parenting and will bridge the gap between what you know and what you do.

How you were parented is the largest single factor in how you will parent. Remembered feelings and experiences will help parents and teachers become less afraid of each other so we can work together to help children keep their curiosity, creativity, and sense of wonder.

The Pitcher Theory

The one common, yet very unique, thing we bring to our parenting is ourselves. One of the best ways to help your child is to understand something I call "the parent pitcher."

The parent pitcher concept is simple. Let's say you are a pitcher and for a normal day your pitcher holds a certain amount of love, time, energy, and nurturing. Your kids, your spouse, the neighbors, work, church, the PTO, and whatever else, are the glasses. Now it is the pitcher's job to fill glasses, right? How many glasses must your pitcher fill? If there is enough in the pitcher, your job is a snap. But what if there's nothing in the pitcher? You can't fill those glasses regardless of how hard you try.

What is in your parent pitcher? We all have days when our pitcher is low or empty. Frustration really sets in when you find you have nothing more to give. Who's in charge of keeping the pitcher full?

You are responsible for keeping your pitcher full. You are responsible for staying aware of your pitcher and keeping your pitcher healthy. Watch for additions and subtractions from your pitcher. Get out of your rut, rest, exercise, and go with the positive.

Few people get everything they need for their pitcher from others. Filling your own pitcher is taking care of the self of you. We have to find ways of nurturing our own needs as well as those of our children.

One mother did not like or enjoy the violin. Then she went to the symphony and heard an ensemble. She discovered she loved the sound of a violin. It now fills her pitcher.

Parents giving power to children is really important. If not given appropriately, they will get it inappropriately.

External factors can control you only if you permit them. If you have to stand in line, how you decide to do it is completely up to you. You can read, write a letter, bring a coloring book, etc.

Let's say a wife is at home and her pitcher has run low. When her husband comes home from work, he offers to fold the clothes, do the dishes, and then take the kids to the park for an hour or so. Do you think she will begin to feel a little better?

But what if her husband comes home complaining about a terrible day at the office and announces he's going to take a shower and go straight to bed? Now we have two empty parent pitchers. The husband can't fill his wife's pitcher if his is empty, too. So, while it is possible for someone else to fill your pitcher, as an adult you are ultimately responsible for filling your own pitcher.

Can you identify when your pitcher runs low under what circumstances? It is very important to be aware of your pitcher level. If you can determine how you feel when your pitcher is full, and what happens when it is empty, then you can take charge of your life, your self-esteem, and keep your pitcher filled to a comfortable level.

In every parenting workshop I lead, we discuss the parent pitcher concept, and I ask the class to suggest ways to fill the empty pitcher. The responses I've received over the years would be enough to fill a book! Get creative!

It is easy to fill your pitcher with simple things.

A young man in college was majoring in agriculture. He was going to spend the summer with a farmer for his laboratory requirement. When he arrived, the farmer was milking a cow. The farmer said, "Hello son, you are right on time." The student replied, "How can you tell time by milking a cow? That is so great—unbelievable. I hope I will be able to do that." The farmer replied, "You can do it. It's really easy. Get down here under the cow. Grab an udder. Now look over at the clock on the wall and you will know the time." Simple usually works best. There is a lot to be said in favor of simplicity. Sometimes we ease into a simpler life by moving forward, not backward.

Every individual has a hobby or personal activity that brings relaxation and peace of mind.

They make you feel fresh and refueled. Activities such as rest, exercise, needlework, or gardening are good, proven pitcher fillers.

It is OK to have an empty pitcher for a while. That is what family is for: strength, support, and human Band-Aids. You must learn how to move your pitcher from empty to full. One of the hardest things to learn is that I am not a scared, helpless person; I can make my pitcher full again.

There are other great fillers for your parent pitcher. Have you gotten out of your rut and done something impossible lately? I stuck my tongue out once at an Olin Mills family photo shoot. Jay took a Rubik Cube apart and left the pieces on the kitchen table. When he had no other clean socks, he wore his red Christmas ones with green trees in July! He didn't care. None of us did. We enjoyed those minor magic moments and rewired a few routine neurons in our brains.

Try getting out of your rut. Shop on a different day, get out of bed on the other side, take a Wednesday off, drive a different way to work, serve spaghetti for breakfast if you must! A change in routine can do wonders for your outlook, help you feel in charge of your life, conquer helplessness, and fill your pitcher.

Another helpful suggestion for filling your pitcher is to balance what I call "additions and subtractions." If you have a carpool, Little League, and church obligations as glasses for your pitcher to fill, you'll be running on empty too quickly, unless you can subtract the PTO and watching your neighbor's kids on Thursday night. If you are aware of your pitcher, you will be aware of your limitations and can easily balance your additions and subtractions. And by keeping your pitcher mostly full, you will feel better about yourself and your role as a parent.

I want to share a story by Charles Lelly that I use in my classes:

> *The art of living consists of knowing what to keep and what to throw away as excess baggage. Living the beautiful way of life calls for a discriminating choice of wonders at your beck and call. You choose those wonders that build you up, not those that tear you down. You choose only those things that fulfill your own very special needs. You have become a master in the art of being and building yourself. You always maintain a firm hold on the rudder of your life ship. But you must steer a course toward the goal of your choosing. You recognize the*

essence within you and selectively seek its reunion in the world about you.

Turn Down Your Background Tapes

We already know the most important thing we bring to our parenting is ourselves. We also understand that children model our behavior, and know it is important that we feel good about ourselves and our parenting.

Some adults still feel uncomfortable in school, even those who are active in the PTO or are volunteers. This "we/they" relationship has been reinforced over time. People only came to school when their kids were in trouble. We need to support kids within a partnership. This means that we adults need to get in touch with our insecurities about our own schooling, so we no longer unconsciously and subtly pass them on to our children.

Parents today are very concerned with studying the latest up-to-the-minute advice, approaches, and attitudes on parenting. We watch the talk shows, read relevant articles, and even books like this one. Yet, despite the wealth of advice available, we raise our children much as we were raised. Why? Because past experiences were recorded in our heads without question along with clear feelings such as love and fear. These background tapes of our childhood experiences play stronger and louder than the newly acquired information we read in books.

When my husband was in the Air Force and we traveled from base to base, we used to attend a lot of potluck suppers to get acquainted. At one particular event, I was asked to bring deviled eggs. I worked hard to make a nice big tray full of deviled eggs for the party. When we were at the party in the supper line, I was embarrassed to hear two ladies wonder, "Who brought those eggs?" I thought about keeping my mouth shut, but I was afraid something may be wrong with the eggs, so I owned up to the fact that I made them. When I claimed the eggs, one of the ladies said they were delicious, but just looked funny. She had never seen them cut crosswise instead of lengthwise.

For years I had wondered why my deviled eggs always rolled around on the platter. And how many times do you suppose I have eaten deviled eggs cut the "right" way at other functions? Probably just short of a million or so—lots of potluck suppers in the Air Force, you know. Yet it had never occurred to me that there was a better way to cut the eggs in half. The following Christmas at my mother's house brought it all together for me.

She passed a platter of deviled eggs around the table and, sure enough, they were cut crosswise.

Whether you are analyzing the way you cut your eggs or the way you deal with your children, most times you will find yourself using techniques your parents used. This is not necessarily bad. Perhaps your parents used some very effective techniques. What is essential is for you to analyze each technique as an understanding adult, keeping those you like and discarding those you don't.

Remember, too, that your children are in apprenticeships to be parents. What will their background tapes play for *them* when they become parents? Much like looking in a mirror, this realization alone can be enough incentive for you to modify your behavior appropriately! So, turn down your background tapes, analyze your parenting methods, then keep what works and lose what doesn't.

Picking the Prom Dress

Just as parenting finds us acting like our parents did, you will find that being a parent gives you a second chance at being a child. Or better said, having another crack at becoming yourself.

I have a friend who truly blossomed in college but was quite the wallflower in high school and never attended a school dance. Consequently, when her daughter was invited to the junior prom, my friend was ecstatic. They set out immediately to buy her prom dress, and you can probably imagine the rest. Living vicariously through her daughter, my friend insisted on a dress she liked best and naturally an argument resulted. Really, whose prom was it?

Do you live all your children's experiences, good and bad, as if they were your own? This is what makes parenting so difficult. Getting another crack at being yourself means dealing with your background tapes. But as an adult, you must learn to let your child pick her own prom dress.

There is a trick to using this skill in your parenting. You will be most successful if you remember what it feels like to be a child, then avoid acting like one. And remember, don't feel guilty about feeling good. You don't have to suffer to be successful as a parent.

Four Basic Parenting Principles

In order to be a good parent and bring your child to adulthood, you must, at some point, practice four basic parenting principles. I've named them:

Love No Matter What
Just Listen
Fences and Consequences
Don't Go Out in the Rain

These principles help us toward our goal of raising self-sufficient adults.

Love No Matter What

The first principle is unconditional love. Learn to love your children, no matter what. I always tell my children, "I love you no matter what!" My daughter came to me and said, "What if I made all Fs. Would you still love me no matter what?" My answer reminded her that flunking was a problem, and we would have to do something about it, but yes, I would love her even if she made all Fs. She's started college now, and I still say to her, "I love you even if you make all Fs." That sentence has special meaning for us.

"No matter what" means you will love unconditionally. You *must* give unconditional love to bring your child to adulthood. You *must* believe in unconditional love, and you *must* practice it. And the first person to start with is *yourself.*

Just Listen

The second basic principle is listening to your child, listening to his feelings whether you agree with them or not. *People cannot become true adults until they know their feelings. An adult who knows how to move out of his feelings will then be able to care for others.* If you know how you feel, you become a much better listener, as well.

Listening with focused attention is one of the greatest forces for change. If someone believes in my words, they believe in me. Then I can believe in myself.

Listening to feelings, as well as words, is very important. All feelings are OK. They are not good or bad, they're just there. All feelings are acceptable to a trusted listener. The behavior resulting from a feeling, however, is another thing altogether.

Many people think that if you have a feeling, you must immediately act on it. This is not true. Usually, if you can get the feeling out, you will deal with it positively. Otherwise, the feeling is inside and is not "dealable," and has unrealistic, magnified power. We must acknowledge our children's feelings, as well as our own, in order to teach them how to deal with their emotions.

There is a very important four-letter word I like. It is *wait*. Don't expect too much too soon. Don't try and push children into behavior they are not ready for. It spoils the fun for children and parents. Whatever you do, if you meet with too much resistance, ask yourself if you are pushing your child too far, too fast. When a child feels he is given time to grow, invariably he will relax and begin to blossom.

We need to have faith in our child's innate capacity to change. Accept where they are and focus on the good they can become. *It takes a lot of slow to grow.* Step back and let the child experience his strength. When you want to work on something in a family or with a particular child, decide on one or two specifics and don't tackle the whole ball of wax. Tell your child, "I love you when you are growing, when you fall back, and when you surge ahead."

I remember hearing a story that demonstrates this concept. Molly was six and Cindy was three. It was Cindy's birthday and Molly had been a tremendous helper at the party. Molly watched her little sister receive all sorts of presents, including a Barbie horse. Molly was dying to have a Barbie horse, but she continued to help with cake and ice cream for Cindy's friends.

After the guests went home, her mother had to start dinner and Molly had spelling words to practice. But instead, Molly began to bicker with Cindy and tried to take away the Barbie horse. She was jealous. Cindy had received all the attention and the gifts. Sibling rivalry was in full force.

Finally, her mother sat down and said to Molly, "Sit with me and talk to me. It sounds like you're feeling kind of jealous. Do you wish that Barbie horse was yours"? Molly didn't quite know what to say, so she answered, "Yeah." Mother said, "You know I've felt jealous before. Last week I saw a blouse my friend had, and it was pretty. I wished I could have it." She continued, "You'll learn to manage. Feelings of jealousy aren't awful. People feel jealous and it's OK. You will learn to manage your feelings, to stop feeling jealous, and to work hard and save money for the things you want. And I'll help you." You know what Molly did? She studied her spelling and had a good night.

So often, what do we say in a situation like this? "You're older, you're bigger. It's Cindy's birthday, not yours. Leave her new toys alone." All this does is make the child deny her feelings and feel more jealous. And it doesn't teach a thing about taking charge of your emotions, which is adult behavior.

What's really important in this story is her mother's reaction. She listened to what Molly was saying and feeling. Her mother had to accept her own past feelings of jealousy. She had to acknowledge that jealousy is a human trait, and that it's an OK way to feel. Her daughter saw this acceptance, knew it was real, then put her energy into spelling.

You see, we can only help our children accept their feelings to the degree we have accepted our own.

Here is a simpler example, one of patient and careful listening, in my own family. Ben was probably five or six years old when Jay renewed his subscription to *Time* magazine. If he renewed for two years, he got a free 35 mm camera. Importantly, the film camera was all plastic. Perfect, Jay thought, for an introduction to photography for Ben.

When the camera came, Jay was more excited than Ben, wanting to establish a hobby both could share over the years. Ben dutifully accepted the camera and a roll of film, and Jay waited. He waited, confident that Ben would seek his expert advice.

Ben did come to him, but he said, "Dad, the guest bathroom is not flushing right." Sure enough, Jay found incomplete flushing, an embarrassment for any visitors. Ever the aspiring handyman, he reached down as deep as he could and felt something, something like plastic.

He wondered, then sighed, then asked, "Ben, did you flush that camera down the toilet?" "No, Dad." Jay accepted what Ben said because he trusted his son, and Ben knew it.

Now Ben felt bad. He came to Jay a little later and said, "Dad, I think I might have."

Jay couldn't dislodge the object. His felt his pride wobble when he had to call a plumber and pay for what he tried to do.

"Yeah, Dad, I flushed it," Ben said, and he felt better. Jay said nothing, just nodded, and felt better for his son.

Our house was a corner lot on the main road of our subdivision in Manchester. We had lots of traffic to and from work. Now our toilet was upside down on the front lawn for all the world to see.

The plumber broke the camera apart in quick time and reinstalled the toilet. Jay told us he learned something new: a heavy wax donut seals the porcelain base to plumbing in the floor so there are no leaks.

Jay was my quiet hero that day, and so was our son. Jay practiced what I taught my parents — patient and careful listening without judgment of the child. To solve the problem, all Jay really did was *just listen*.

It was February 29, 1987, and Ben was 10½. He wanted to stay home and not go to the baseball pitching and hitting clinic at St. Louis Community College-Meramec. We discussed how he felt. He said he could take either hitting or pitching but really didn't want to do either one. He wanted to play with Chandler this afternoon. We discussed that knowing his feelings was the most important thing. It's important to say how you feel even if you don't get what you want. Ben was afraid he would disappoint Jay. I asked Ben, "Do you want me to tell Daddy?" He pointed his finger at me to tell him.

When Jay came home, I was in the bathroom. Jay asked Ben if he wanted to go to baseball. Ben said he hadn't decided yet. (He was waiting for me to talk to Jay.)

Jay told Ben that knowing your own feelings is more important and it is OK sometimes to not feel like going to baseball. Jay said sometimes he did not feel like going to the baseball clinic either, because he had to wait 1½ hours and take along any book he could grab. Ben had never considered that Jay didn't want to go, or that going could be extra effort for him.

Listening to shared feelings is fundamental to personal growth and trust between people.

I want to tell you a fable that Abraham Lincoln told as more food for thought. It is an old fable about the competition between the North Wind and the Sun to make a man take off his coat. The North Wind blew as hard as it could to blow the coat off, but the man just pulled his coat more tightly around him. The colder and harder the North Wind blew, the tighter he pulled his coat. However, the Sun with its slow, gentle radiance warmed the man. When he relaxed and felt comfortable enough, he took off his coat.

The raising and educating of children follow exactly the same principle. The way to encourage your child to open up to his own possibilities and the fullness of his life is by surrounding him with your warm and gentle radiance. Listen, then wait.

If the piano recital is two weeks away and your child says she knows the piece, but we say keep working on it, we discourage the child from her own confidence that fills her own pitcher.

Sheila had lost a lot of weight and her boss was going to meet her at a big conference in Florida. She couldn't find a dress for the occasion. Before this, Sheila would be saying . . . *if only I could lose weight!* Now she is saying she can't find a dress and still looks terrible in a bathing suit.

There is always a way to drag ourselves down, use our energy non-productively, and suffer. Recognize when your inner critic talks, then promptly slay it! As A. A. Milne's Christopher Robin said, "Doing nothing is doing something. It's listening to all the things you can't hear, and not bothering."

Fences and Consequences

The third parenting principle concerns external controls. To help your child become an adult, you must provide sufficient and consistent external controls until the child learns to incorporate such controls within himself.

Researchers have found that kids in a fenced playground will run and play almost endlessly. But if you take the fence down, the children become apprehensive. They no longer know where the boundaries are. They haven't learned enough to decide for themselves.

Children need parameters. They need external controls for equilibrium and for a sense of security as they learn what is called logical consequences.

Understanding logical consequences, that if I do this, then this will happen, is a very important step toward adulthood. To foster this understanding, you as a parent must establish the parameters (but not too many), then follow through and enforce them. The key is this, do what you say you're going to do!

If you tell your child, "You are not going to eat any more potato chips today," then do not let the child have another potato chip. If you do, then the child will realize he can push a little harder and then a little harder until you give in.

Many parents get upset at this, arguing that they said something stupid or something they shouldn't have said. This happens to all of us. Work hard on your follow through. Even consistently enforced bad judgment is more valuable to the child then a poorly enforced good one. It shows by example that adults are imperfect, too!

When you don't follow through on what you say, your children get confused about their power and terrible struggles will result. A child who expects logical consequences from his actions, instead of arbitrary punishment, will learn a lot more about himself and life.

A boy in a nearby elementary school set the dumpster on fire as a prank. The teachers and parents alike were outraged and called for the principal to expel the boy from school. The principal, however, knew the boy would not learn much from this. He chose to deal with the boy using logical consequences instead of punishment. The boy had exhibited a lack of respect for school property. To teach him respect for the property of others, the principal ordered the boy to assist the school janitor every day after school for two weeks.

The result was very positive. The young boy had been lonely after school and looking for trouble, but by assisting the janitor, the boy learned a lot, worked hard, and made a new adult friend.

When Ben was a barely a toddler, he was as curious and adventurous as any. One day, he was in the kitchen with me. I thought he was ready, so I introduced him to a box of raisins. This was my first attempt with finger foods that he could choke on. He managed well as I puttered around. *Success!* I thought.

Later in the day, Ben developed sniffles and I didn't connect the dots. This continued the next day, but he didn't have the other symptoms of a cold. Hmm. Interesting. Then the light went on.

I asked him, "Ben, did you put a raisin up your nose yesterday?" He replied, "Yes. My nose was hungry." I looked up his nostrils and saw a dark blob and was able to wiggle it out. Then I said, "Ben, raisins are for your mouth and no other place, OK? Do you understand?" He looked a little sheepish, but said, "Yes." But as the day went on, he continued to sniffle and snort.

I got a flashlight and some tweezers, then asked Ben to let me look at his nose again. Sure enough, I pulled out three more thoroughly ripe and plump raisins, all coated in pale green snot. In a matter of minutes, Ben was back to just being Ben.

"What did you learn from this, Ben?" I asked. He replied, "Umm, raisins are just for eating." I said, "And what happens when you put them up your nose?" My son said, "Your nose gets angry." I nodded, "And angry noses can make you sick, too."

The important lesson here for parents and teachers is to look beyond what is happening and look at what's being learned. And remember, following through and helping your child to incorporate logical consequences within his or her sense of self is a true form of loving.

Don't Go Out in the Rain

We have agreed on the importance of unconditional love, listening and accepting feelings, and the need to provide loving and consistent external parameters until our children can incorporate boundaries within themselves.

The fourth basic principle of parenting is to let your child learn to make his own decisions.

A story I use to illustrate this is called "Don't Go Out in the Rain." When dealing with your toddler, you have to say, "Don't go out in the rain," because he doesn't understand why he should or shouldn't. You can talk about the rain, or you can put on his raincoat and boots and let him go walking in the rain, or just scoop your child up and say, "Can't go out today." To the toddler, your decision is final.

As the child grows a little older, perhaps three or four years old, he is moving toward making a few more decisions on his own. If you say, "Don't go out in the rain," he will still want to do it because he wants to break away from you. Try to give him some power over the rain. Say, "Gee, if we wait until after lunch it will be warmer, and we could go out for 10 minutes." Or you may say, 'Let's call

Time and Temperature and see if it's too cold to go out in the rain."

When you say "don't go out in the rain" to the elementary school child, you may find she goes out anyway. Or she may refuse to take her raincoat. An elementary school child is old enough to play in the rain, dry off, and put away a raincoat.

Let your child have consequences as much as possible. You may say, "It's awfully cold out there and I'm not sure you should go out in the rain." If he chooses to go out anyway, he may come back in and say, "Golly, you were right. It really is chilly out there. I hope I don't catch a cold." Then you will see his development of internal logical consequences.

Often, parents are on their child's case all the time, saying, "Don't you have more sense than that? I told you so!" Your child will learn much quicker if you let him find out on his own what he should and shouldn't do. Sometimes, they may not need what we think they need.

I know I've gone places as a child and adults have told me to bundle up, but I was hot and didn't need to bundle up. I knew my own body.

The best approach with the elementary school kid is to say, "We're going to play soccer and it's raining. It might start to pour. What do you think we should carry?" Then support your child when it stops raining by saying, "You can leave your raincoat in the trunk."

"Don't go out in the rain" at this stage is really about letting the child make as many decisions as possible. In this way, the child will grow strong and internalize these rights and wrongs. You will see your child able to solve problems and filled with a good sense of self-esteem.

Many parents complain to me that their teenagers can't make decisions. Often this is because they did it all for them at an earlier stage!

Adolescence is the last stage before adulthood. When you say "don't go out in the rain" to the adolescent, you better be prepared to accept the fact he will do whatever he wants. The very nature of this stage of development is to go against you, the parent. If you can't handle this fact, you're going to have a hard time.

Adolescence is really the stage of transitioning the existing relationship of parent and child to friend and friend. This process sees the adolescent move through three phases: three-fourths child and one-fourth adult, to one-half child and one-half adult, and then to one-fourth child and three-fourths adult. As your child moves closer to being an adult, he is separating from you.

This is our goal as parents: to raise a separate and self-sufficient adult, a Fully Functioning Human Being, an FFHB. But if you're still relating to every triumph and every hurt of theirs as if your child is still five years old, you are not separating.

Separation means that you remain a loving presence, available if needed, but otherwise just watch the show go by. Allowing separation also means not being disturbed if the child makes a mistake that wiser adults would avoid.

It's OK during adolescence to say, "don't go out in the rain" and see your child want to do the very opposite. Just make sure your position is firm. Every self-respecting 16-year-old knows what his family stands for and the values you have instilled. He knows what you appreciate and what you don't like.

"Don't go out in the rain" is most beautiful, I think, when you express it to your adult child as an observation. The power struggle has passed. By this stage, you and your child have connected as friend to friend. Your child now responds as an adult and understands, "My parents love me very much. They have a lot to share and a lot to offer. And so do I." As a true adult, your child can listen to other people, including you, and make his own valuable decisions because you taught him to live from his own internal meaning and feelings.

Support Systems

I define the adult we all want to be as a Fully Functioning Human Being, an FFHB, someone who can grow from his own inner feelings to truly care for others. What people were good for you when growing up? What kind of traits did they have? How did you feel around them? People who are good for us help us feel good about being separate individuals.

I must emphasize that self-responsibility doesn't mean that you or your child have no need of support. The support of your family and those close to you is not just nice, it is essential.

Likewise, support and commitment to your child will do more for him then anything money can buy. As a parent, you will encounter a variety of problems in their growing years, but commitment to your child will help you to see beyond the current conflict to the positive qualities you know exist in your child.

Your support to the child is not just nice, it is essential. What support do they need? What support do they receive? How do you, at the same time, provide support for the rest of your family? How do you, at the same time, get support from your family?

Needs Vs. Wants

Support requires a sensitivity to individual needs. An individual's needs are indeed determined by the individual, and parents, teachers, or society cannot always tell a child what he needs.

Being a child today is very complicated because of all the choices available. Lots of choices call for a higher level of thinking then does one or two alternatives. If we ask too much of our children, or present too many choices, the child may become overloaded, and the result is stress. Teach your child to plan ahead and explain how plans sometimes change.

Have you ever considered why kids love fast food restaurants? They know the choices are easy. Even parents usually would prefer to drive through one when they are tired, rather than go to a French restaurant. Making decisions requires a higher level of thinking. Neither adults nor children can always maintain a high level of thinking.

Parents must be careful of thinking children can do it all or have to try to do it all. Your child needs you in a strong adult role to take charge and support him by discussing his choices. The child does not have to join or participate in everything. You need to let him know you don't expect it! This kind of support will do more for your child than anything money can buy.

Characteristics of a Nurturing Family

Human feelings and human life are more important than anything else. People who nurture know that things take time. You can't plant a seed in the morning and expect to pick a flower in the afternoon. Foresters often plant orchards and never see the full-grown trees. Instead, they find patience and enjoyment in the planting.

Here are some characteristics of a nurturing family — one that builds self-esteem:

> **Nurturing families show affection and feel comfortable touching each other. Studies show that infants die if not touched.**

> **Nurturing families look each other in the eye at eye level and call each other by name. Nurturing parents**

are polite and keep things simple. This releases stress and shows that we care about another's feelings.

Nurturing families talk openly about feelings, about each other's needs and desires, about anything. No one is a mind reader. Go with the positive and keep your sense of humor.

Nurturing families accept change as an unavoidable part of being alive. Change often takes time. Change can make you feel in charge and gets you out of a rut.

Nurturing families are flexible. They stretch their thinking and bounce back.

Let It Go

Sometimes, situations call for supporting the child rather than scolding. If you are a blamer, you are teaching your child blame rather than seeking a solution. React in proportion to the behavior: spilled milk is not the same as a wrecked car.

I had a neighbor who watched a nest of robin eggs hatch in a bush outside her front door. She and her seven-year-old daughter enjoyed looking at the baby birds. One day, for whatever reason, the little girl squirted the baby birds with water when she was playing. Soon thereafter the birds died. When my neighbor questioned her daughter as to why the birds might have died, the child broke down in sobs and confessed to squirting the birds.

She could have punished her daughter verbally by calling it inhumane behavior. Instead, she sensed the girl's sincere sorrow and offered support. Sometimes, situations call for supporting the child rather than scolding.

The mother told her daughter she must bury the birds and offered to help. Together, they dug a hole in the back yard and at the same time talked about death. Then the mother explained how we, as humans, must take care of smaller creatures and those humans who cannot take care of themselves.

When they were done with their discussion, my neighbor let the incident go. The child will never again make that mistake. They talked about what was learned, and then they let it go.

There are many good books on death available for children, like *Annie and the Old One* by Miska Miles. Kids often understand death better if they learn it first when a creature or pet dies, before they experienced the loss of a human.

Child Choices

Children need to have things they can control and the opportunity to act out their life as they understand it. For example, give your child some interesting junk and ask, "Can you make something of this?" Then see what she does.

When my son, Ben, was nine, he had the following choices, all in one day. Number one was to work on his Science Fair project because he decided to do a complicated battery experiment; number two was to work on his God and Country award for Cub Scouts; number three was to finish building his car for the Pinewood Derby, a big deal in our area; number four was to play with his friends in the neighborhood, important to Ben; and number five was to watch a program on TV he had been waiting to see. These are heavy-duty choices for a boy of nine to make!

The derby was a big thing and working on the car takes a lot of time, while playing and just running around doing your own thing is also needed. The Science Fair was important because it also took a lot of his time. Too many choices call for a higher level of thinking. That is overload and creates stress. Children need strong adults to discuss choices that they want to do. We must look again at what we are asking of our children.

Parent Guidelines for Child Creativity

Some people say that the true purpose of education is to help the child find what they really love to do so they can live a life of beauty and creativity with a sense of wonder.

A child's play is his work. Play is learning by doing. They encounter life in structured and unstructured play. They process, learn, and give back in play.

Play is hard work, their work. Watching them play helps us parents learn what the child knows and what the child understands. Knowing is not the same as understanding. A child may be able to count to a hundred, yet not be able to fetch four napkins for the table.

Here are some ideas for enriching a child's creative capacity for play:

Create a non-threatening atmosphere.

Teach the child to observe.

Ask the child what he/she wonders about.

Provide toys that stimulate imagination.

Provide a variety of materials
that can be manipulated.

Avoid art materials that limit imagination.

Keep in mind that the process
is more important than the product.

Encourage natural abilities and self-expression:
dancing, music, writing, etc.

Tolerate errors and show your child
how to learn from the gift of mistakes.

Ask open ended questions.

Parent Choices

It is very important that we don't hang labels on children and tell them how special they are because, when we do that, we are telling them that they have a different set of criteria for judging themselves. If they're so special that what is right for other people isn't right for them, they put enormous pressure on themselves.

We need to just let children be themselves. They are unique and we do love them, but this special business is causing us to create a different set of expectations for them.

One of the hard things about parenting today is that children and parents have so many things to choose from: so many toys, so many stores, so many dolls, so many cans of soup.

Be careful of thinking your child has to do it all. Adults need to take charge and support their children's choices. The child does not have to join and participate in everything. We need to let them know that! Adults must not expect the child to do it all.

Many of these projects need to be done at school, not as homework. Everything the child needs for the Science Fair should be at school so they can work on it at school. Use a whole morning, whole day, or whole week in school to do your project using the teacher as a resource.

The teacher must not say that you've got to do all of the project at home and your parents have to help you and buy all this stuff. One reason kids like short rest periods is because they make choices easily when rested, but not when they are really tired.

Making a lot of choices is high level thinking. Adults as well as children can't always maintain that high level of thinking. Children will be very motivated and want to do a project if they have a project that's interesting and the resources are provided for them. To have to go out on your own after you've been in school all day and hunt all this stuff down is too much for our children.

We need to have in school every book, every pamphlet, every video, every hands-on thing, every resource the child needs, and that is the teacher's job. Use the teacher as a resource to help the child do research during school. Then homework is continuing what you did all day, just in a different room.

When I was a teacher, I can recall being aggravated by parents who persisted and literally nagged me about a child's particular problem or progress. But even so, I had to admit that at least the child had someone committed to him. When all is said and done, nothing is more valuable to a child than the support of Mom and Dad. Everybody who has ever made it in this world has had *someone* who was there for them.

Mixed Messages

This advice came from *Better Homes and Gardens* in 1986 and I always made a copy for my parenting classes. Here is a condensation of what the article said.

These are the top mixed messages parents send children and their remedies:

The Zap: "This is a great report card. Why can't you do this well all the time?" The Tease: "We'll see. I'll think about it." (They really mean No.)

The Wheedle: "I could use some help with the groceries. You think you could tear yourself away from the TV and lend me a hand?" (Just say, "I need help with the groceries right now.")

The Shuttle: Mom says, "Go ask Dad." Dad says, "What did your mother say?" Don't avoid confrontation and teach your child to be manipulative. Just say Yes or No or "We'll let you know after we talk."

The Switch: This is the old-fashioned double standard. Dad says, "It's wrong to cheat in school." But he brags to his friends about fudging on his tax return. Clean up your own act first, parent.

The Quick Change: Condoning behavior on one occasion and punishing it on another is one form. Another form is punishing big for small mistakes and punishing small for big ones. Be consistent with your expectations and consequences. And always follow through.

Parenting Myths

These myths are from Arthur Combs:

Kids won't learn unless you make them. This is the result of an irrelevant school curriculum. Students are not motivated to learn because they see no meaning in the material. 'I'll never use geometry after I graduate, so what's the point?' Now the teacher faces an unwilling learner and feels pressured to make him learn. This creates a disastrous circle and confirms the myth. When students feel challenged, they respond. An example is learning to roller skate.

Kids will learn difficult things without coercion if it is relevant to their needs at the time, if it is tailored to their ability to learn, and it is both interesting and personally rewarding.

If it's hard for you, it's good for you. It's not hard if it is challenging and has relevance to the child's life.

CHAPTER 2:
BUILDING SELF ESTEEM

What Is Self-Esteem?

What is self-esteem? Self-esteem is simply how you feel about yourself. Generally, however, this definition is too straightforward for some people. We look for something more technical and concrete to help us understand this vague phenomenon.

The concept of self-esteem is like a tree. The branches reach out in proportion to the depths of the roots. If a tree has shallow roots, it will topple when the branches reach out too far. If the tree is deeply rooted in the ground, it can support and balance the branches no matter how far they reach.

It is worth repeating: self-respect is the hallmark of self-esteem.

A child whose feelings of inner sureness are deeply rooted will have great ability to reach out, grow, develop, and learn. Such a child will also be able to recognize the worth of others.

Children with poor self-esteem feel inadequate inside. There is a lack of harmony and balance and comfort in their lives. Disease is defined as any harmful or destructive condition. Let us here reconsider the word disease as DIS-EASE.

Few things can be as destructive to your developing child as a weak sense of self-esteem. Strong self-esteem, on the other hand, provides comfort, balance, and harmony to the inner self, and this security is the core to all we do in our lives.

Still, what is self-esteem? I've asked children in my classes, "If you make good grades, do you have good self-esteem? How about if you are pretty? If you are rich, will you feel good about yourself?" Kids often think so. But we know this is usually not the case. We often read about Hollywood and the rich and beautiful, but miserable, people. Self-esteem has very little to do with what is on the outside (like looks, wealth, and talents), nor is self-esteem a magical end to all problems.

I believe good self-esteem has more to do with this inner sureness we've been talking about. Self-esteem is a feeling of self-worth and value. Good self-esteem is believing in yourself; it breeds self-confidence and the belief that you can truly handle whatever challenges life presents, whatever problems come along. This doesn't mean you won't be confronted with a situation you don't like, but if you have the confidence to handle the problem and do what you need to do and move on, you will have a good sense of self.

Consider the following examples.

I Can Handle It

Children can and should learn to handle problems at a very young age. When my son, Ben, was in the first grade, his favorite part of the day was coming home. He was not really crazy about school and looked forward to playing outdoors.

One particular afternoon, the kids on the school bus got a bit rowdy and the bus driver threatened to stop the bus and put the kids out on the street. Well, Ben didn't care for this idea at all and by the time he got home he was full of tears and determined never to ride the bus to school again.

So, we talked about the situation. First, I assured him that the law would not allow the bus driver to just put him off the bus on a busy street where he couldn't find his way home which, of course, is what he feared. Then we talked about how the bus driver might turn the bus around and take the kids back to school. Ben said he wouldn't want to go back to school, and he might cry. I asked him, what could he do?

Ben thought he could go to his classroom and find his teacher and then he wouldn't be scared. He also thought he could go to the school office and call me to come get him. Either way, I told Ben, he may not like the situation, and he may have some tears, but he could handle it. And after our discussion, Ben understood he could handle it, too.

Mistakes Are Okay, Everything Is As It Should Be

Another indicator of good self-esteem is the ability to handle mistakes. Humans make mistakes and you need to let your children know it is OK to mess up now and then.

I remember another incident with Ben. I believe he was three or four years old. I was rushing to get ready for an appointment and just as we were about to leave, Ben decided to help himself to a cherry from the jar in the refrigerator. As a toddler is apt to do, he spilled the whole jar and I had cherry juice running down the inside of my refrigerator. What a mess! But at the moment, I did not have time to deal with the spill, so I scooped Ben up and said, "We will clean this up later. People make mistakes."

Children at this age have no sense of time, no idea of "hurry." I'm embarrassed to admit it, but I was so busy I had to tolerate the cherry juice for a full week before I got around to cleaning up. By then, it was dried and sticky, and I had to scrape it off with a knife. All the while, Ben was watching me clean. I gave him a rag to help, and he said, "Mom, tell me about making mistakes again."

Ben was saying a week later (an eternity at his age), "Is it *still* OK to make mistakes? Are you mad at me *now*? Have you changed your mind, Mom, about mistakes? That was a big mess to me! I forgot how big!"

I was amazed my simple statement had stuck with him, and we had a very nice talk about learning from our mistakes. We even thought of different ways to store the cherries so as to avoid spilled cherry juice in the future. *Improvement is more valuable than perfection.* What is being learned is more valuable than what is happening.

The lesson for us as parents is to be patient with mistakes and not place blame. This teaches a powerful preventive lesson to our kids that has no immediate payoff. How you react to mistakes will teach your children a lot. I call this the "Power Over the Mouth" concept. What will your child think if you react as emotionally to spilled milk as you do to a wrecked car? Remember to look beyond what is happening to what's being learned. In almost every case, the lesson is that making mistakes is OK!

Never Criticize Or Compare

A favorite author of mine, R. Buckminster Fuller, says in his book, *4D Time Lock*, "All children are born geniuses, and we spend the first six years of their lives de-geniusing them." In my experience as a mother and teacher, we do that by criticizing them for making mistakes.

Criticism is a trap for many parents.

If there is one rule you take with you from my teaching, please let it be this: NEVER criticize your child or compare his personal uniqueness to someone else. Criticism destroys self-esteem. You can analyze incorrect *behavior*, you can encourage your child to try a better way to do something, but criticism of the *person* will never give you the results you are seeking.

Comparing your child to another one is equally destructive. It is also extremely unfair. Every child is unique with his or her special set of strengths and weaknesses. When you compare your child to another, you are ignoring her good points and evaluating according to another person's standards or strengths, creating winners and losers. Consequently, the child feels unworthy, and self-esteem is lowered. Evaluating a child — or an adult for that matter — requires this comparison.

It is bad enough for the losers to feel unworthy, but even the winners, especially those with low self-esteem, feel the same. They tend to fantasize, "It was just luck. Next time I could lose."

Let your child be himself and appreciate his own unique qualities. By avoiding criticism and comparison, your child will feel better, and so will you. Look at what is being learned, not what happened.

Positive and Negative Talk

Remember, it is the daily little things you say about yourself that really matter. Children hear all the little putdowns and all the pushups. They learn to either use your positive talk or your negative talk. Listen to yourself this week and see what you say to yourself. And learn to love being an adult.

Here's a few examples of things we might tell ourselves to build self-esteem:

I feel good about how I marked the items for the garage sale.

I can live in the present without the past ruling.

I have had problems with meringue for pies, but this time I made it work. The

*new recipe turned out well, and I feel
good.*

And here's a few examples of things that might tear down our self-esteem:

*Oh, we are almost out of gas. I'm so
dumb not to have gotten some.*

*I should have gone to the store
yesterday. I never get what I need at the
store.*

*Stupid me. I can't believe I don't
remember where I parked the car.*

*I never know how to price things for a
garage sale.*

Remember This

I've found that being superhuman is neither realistic nor appreciated. Remember in the pitcher theory that it is OK to sometimes have low points, to have empty pitchers. People with high self-esteem have fewer low points because they understand the concept and forgive themselves when they have an empty pitcher.

Success increases self-esteem by decreasing helplessness, by making trying worthwhile, by providing meaning in the doing, and by making you less afraid of failure. On the other hand, living in the past or letting the future rule you will drain your energy and make you more anxious.

What makes parenting so difficult and hard sometimes? You're getting another crack at being yourself and you're having to deal with your background tapes as they come up.

Empowerment

A child is a person, a human being, although at times he doesn't feel he is. My four-year-old, Ben, was at a restaurant with us looking at the menu. He obviously could not read a menu, but the waiter handed him one anyway and asked him what he wanted. Ben said, "He thinks I'm real!" A child is an autonomous person, a human being, although at times he isn't sure.

Giving power to children is extremely important. Give appropriate power according to the child's age, intelligence, and level of maturity. Never give the child power to alleviate a parent's burden.

Overparenting

Developing good self-esteem is largely tied to the ability to recognize and handle your own problems. Sometimes our children are inhibited by our tendency to do what I call "overparenting." Overparenting is a result of love, wanting only the very best for your children. So, you do everything for them. And everything has to be just right. His shirt must match his slacks, her bow must be tied just so. Most parents recognize the symptoms of overparenting.

Unfortunately, what we do out of love is often not perceived so by our kids. They see overparenting as a message that we don't believe they're capable of figuring something out for themselves. They perceive overparenting as inadequacy on their part, not as love on our part. I know. I overparented deodorant.

When my daughter, Camilla, was in the 5th grade, the teacher did a unit on deodorant at the beginning of the year. She said, "During this year your bodies will be changing, and you will start to use deodorant. So, we are going to do some deodorant research. I want each student to go deodorant shopping, buy the one you like best, and bring it to class."

I have used deodorant for years without much thought, but all of a sudden it was a very big deal. We went to the store and my daughter immediately liked the cute, colorful, fancy bottle.

She was not really interested in which was the best deodorant. Pretty soon, I found myself over-parenting deodorant: telling her this one was too strong, that one wasn't strong enough, and she was going to pay more for the fancy bottle than the plainer one.

Can you believe it? Overparenting deodorant! I was telling her all kinds of things she could figure out for herself. For $2 or whatever, I could have kept my years of deodorant wisdom to myself, and we could have had fun. After all, think what she was learning, think of the power in looking and choosing. The type of deodorant wasn't really important. What was important was her thinking and learning about her changing body plus the stronger sense of self she was developing in the process of considering and deciding what to buy.

Reality Checks

One day I was talking to Lynn, a kindergarten friend of mine, and I said, "My, your brain is really stretching and growing. I can hear you rhyming words you weren't rhyming before. You're saying bat and cat and rat. I can really tell your brain is growing." She turned around and said to me, "My sister says I'm dumb."

I looked her straight in the eye and said, "What do you think?" Talk about a double take! This child exclaimed, "What do *I* think?" like she couldn't believe I would ask her opinion! I repeated my question and explained there would always be people who try to tell her what to think. Others would comment on her abilities. She would have to learn to decide for herself. So, I said again, "What do you think?" And she said, "I'm not so dumb. I'm rhyming."

This brings us to the first point of this story. A child whose parents and teachers listen to her and give encouragement for specific accomplishments will instill in the child a better sense of confidence for her to make up her own mind.

But then I asked Lynn, "What if you're not sure? You think you're OK, but you're not sure because other people are saying you are dumb. What can you do?"

In this case, I told Lynn to go for a reality check. A reality check involves seeking the advice of a "qualified" person, meaning someone who is wise and trustworthy like Mom or Dad or your teacher. Even an older brother of sister could be qualified.

Do You Have Green Hair?

Then I said, "Lynn, you have green hair, yes you do, look at your green hair." She knew she didn't have any green hair, but here I was, a parental authority, saying her hair was green over and over again. Lynn started to doubt, so she ran to the bathroom mirror to check. "I don't have green hair," she said. Then I said, "You understand now what I'm talking about. You checked for yourself and you knew. You must always check for yourself and if you are not sure, you can check with someone you trust who is wise."

Children learn who to believe and who to trust very early. Parents who refrain from criticism, listen to their children, and provide consistent support with specific encouragement, will create that trust in an environment that allows development of a child who is comfortable choosing to believe in herself.

Cushions of Success

If good self-esteem is so essential to the development of your child, you're probably wondering what else you can do to help him feel good about himself.

Feeling good or feeling bad affects what you and your child do today and what both of you learn.

Success is THE MAJOR FORCE in fostering good self-esteem. Sometimes, I run into parents who believe the opposite is true. They say failing makes a child stronger and teaches him to lift himself up like he'll have to do in the unfair, real world. This simply is not true. No child can lift himself up without a base of confidence to lift on. Success builds that base.

Success increases self-esteem several different ways. It gives your child power and independence. It is self-reinforcing. Success is the reward that makes trying and learning worthwhile. Your child can only learn when he is feeling valued and good about himself.

Success also provides what I call "meaning in the doing." When a child can understand and appreciate the importance of the process in his activities, he will find an increased sense of self. Growth is both a knowing and a doing: an understanding and a change in behavior.

Everyone has occasional "down" days, but it is important to remember how feeling good or feeling bad will affect what your child learns. Picture yourself on a "down" day, and then imagine if you were forced to learn Russian on such a day! A second grader who doesn't feel good about himself will have trouble that day learning to add and subtract.

A child can only learn when he is feeling valued and good about himself. So, what you need to do is build some cushions of success for your child to soften the fall of an occasional bad day.

Good self-esteem develops when a child can tackle a task and finish by exclaiming, "I did it!" Success allows your child to demonstrate and feel his growing competence through a variety of life and learning experiences: I did the puzzle; I can skip; I spent the night at camp; I hit a home run; I used my verbs from class; I DID IT! Each I DID IT provides a cushion of success, so to speak. These cushions build up within the child and soften the blow when the child must fail. He can still feel good about himself because he knows he has succeeded in the past and can do it again.

I remember when we repainted the first house we ever bought. It was a big job painting two coats of a pale green color over the chocolate brown. Ben was a toddler and he wanted to help. Jay put a board between two ladders, a board to sit Ben above the ground just a little, just in case he fell.

My husband gave our son an impressive four-inch paint brush like professional painters use, along with an empty paint bucket filled with water. We could see the painting Ben did, because the house was temporarily wet where he painted.

Ben worked with tireless happiness and satisfaction all the way around the house and felt like he contributed as much effort as the rest of the family. We set up a situation with a high probability of success. We didn't need to tell Ben that we valued his help. He knew it.

There are other specific reasons why success is so important to your child:

1. Success gives your child power and independence.

2. Success provides an achievement the child can use at a later date to affirm herself.

3. Success encourages your child to vary his behavior. A child who has been successful will notice if something isn't working and vary his behavior accordingly to achieve success again.

4. Success makes your child less afraid of inevitable failures.

5. Success improves and reinforces the child sense of self with positive thoughts.

6. Success is the reward that makes trying and learning worthwhile.

7. Success counteracts helpless attitudes and feelings.

Building cushions of success requires parents and teachers to actually plan activities and set up situations where the child can succeed. It is crucial to realize that the child can only learn when he is feeling valued and good about himself. In fact, the major difference between a good learner and a poor learner is that the poor learner *feels* he can't do it. The good learner is willing to try because he knows trying *feels* good and may result in success and reward for his effort.

The older your child, the harder it is to set up these situations. This is why it is so imperative for children to meet with success in their early years. From birth to age eight, a child should meet with success most of the time, like 96% success to 4% failure. If a child is not meeting with success most of the time, then something is wrong, and the child stands to suffer for a very long time.

Be Careful of Special

Every child needs to know he is worthy of the love and respect of others, and the child with good self-esteem believes he is. It is very important that we don't hang labels on children and tell them how special they are. When we do that, we are telling them that they have a different set of criteria for judging themselves. If they believe they are so special that what is right for other people isn't right for them, they put enormous pressure on themselves to live up to those unrealistic expectations.

Many well-intentioned parents and teachers use "I am special" lessons aimed at building the child's self-esteem, such as hanging buttons on them, making charts about how special they are, and talking about being special all the time.

Do not saddle your child with being *special* all the time. The child with good self-esteem understands that *special* simply means "unique" and does not mean "superior."

We need to just let children be themselves. Your child must know he's unique and he must feel you love him, but this special business is causing us to create a different set of criteria for ourselves and our kids, namely, I can forgive someone else's mistake, but I can't forgive myself because I'm so special/superior. If you are constantly telling your child how special he is, what he'll hear is that what is right for other people is not right for him, and he'll feel he must live up to superior standards. Then you'll find he puts enormous pressure on himself to live up to his "specialness."

Again, for the healthiest self-esteem, make sure your child knows he is unique and that you love him just being himself.

Productive Vs. Non-Productive Energy

I can't discuss self-esteem, feelings, and their role in parenting without addressing my concept of productive energy. As parents, we need to deal with our own feelings, as well as help our children deal with theirs.

Most people agree that feelings are important. All feelings are legitimate; understanding feelings takes great wisdom.

But many of us were taught that negative feelings are bad and should not be felt. I think feelings are energy, and energy flows. It has to go somewhere regardless of its positive or negative qualities. Talking about feelings always reduces tension. Talking makes feelings easier to deal with. Talking about feelings makes them more manageable and less intense. When a child can't express negative feelings, the most likely result is anti-social behavior, anxiety, or depression.

Your feelings as a parent are very important to acknowledge, too. Do you often say one thing to your child when you feel another? You are not fooling your kids; you are making them distrust their own feelings.

In the course of your life, or better yet the course of your day, you will encounter problems which will take energy to solve. Expect problems, then feel good when you solve them!

Everyone's energy supply is finite, so you'll be more successful if you learn to manage your energy in a productive manner. The more you are successful at this, the better you will feel about yourself. You can't remember what you know when you are under stress.

For example, let's say you need to renew your automobile license plates this month. If you're like most of us, you wake up and think about it every day, worry about getting it done, but continue to put it off. If you're not going to do it today, but you're thinking about doing it, you're wasting your energy. Consequently, you are left with less energy to tackle the projects you want to do today.

I have dealt with this type of problem by designating "D" day on my calendar each month. "D" stands for "DO" and it is the day I save to do all the chores I've been putting off. This way I don't let worry rob my energy every day of the month.

Productive energy allows you to do what you need to do *today*. Living in the past, or letting the future rule you, drains productive energy. If you're living in the past, your tapes are telling you what to do, and you'll find yourself using nonproductive energy to fight the tapes.

Similarly, if you are letting the future rule you, your energy flow is non-productive. Many times, I see parents enroll a child who is not ready into a five-day preschool program. The parents know the child is not ready, but they are afraid if they don't get him in now, he won't be accepted to the *right* kindergarten or even to the *right* college.

If your child is three, let him be three. If she's six, enjoy six. Rest assured the next stage of development will take care of itself.

People with good self-esteem are able to do more with less energy because they know how to do what needs to be done, then move on. You can lead your child to better self-esteem and more productive use of his energy with the proper responses and encouragement.

The daughter of my friend, Mary, has a new baby. She called Mary long distance for advice. It seems the daughter was in night school, her husband was working, and she was concerned about leaving the baby with a sitter because the baby had her first cold. Mary could have added doubt to her daughter's doubt by saying, "It is not a good idea to leave a sick child. Babies are unpredictable and if she really gets congested, she may need her mother."

Or, she could have told her daughter, "Stop being ridiculous and overprotective! All kids get colds and it's really no big deal."

Instead, Mary fed her daughter productive energy, reassuring her that leaving the baby for a few hours with a trusted sitter would be fine. In other words, Mary gave her daughter the energy she needed to go ahead and do what she needed to do, namely go to school.

On the flip side, a few days later I did the opposite and fed my daughter nonproductive energy. Our neighbor was having a garage sale and selling a stereo equalizer. My daughter's boyfriend wanted to buy it, but he also wanted to test it before buying. It occurred to me that the time it took him to test the equalizer was time the machine was "off the floor" lessening the chances of another possible buyer picking it up.

So, I began nagging, "You better hurry, you have to bring that back, etc." I was overparenting again and telling my daughter and her boyfriend I thought they were too stupid to realize on their own they needed to be swift. I was fostering a non-adult relationship with my practically adult child. And I was wasting my own energy worrying about that equalizer.

I have one other thought on the subject of energy. My advice to even the most devoted parents is this: don't put *all your energy* into raising your children, or you will resent them when they leave you, and they will. Instead, model the behavior of a well-rounded parent, a person who can take time off from family responsibilities and tend to personal dreams. Model the kind of parent and adult you hope your child will become.

Finally, don't expect to be appreciated for your good parenting. You can get anything done if you don't care who gets credit!

CHAPTER 3:
KID POWER

Giving Power

Parents, don't think of yourself as a boss, but rather as a guide for your children on their journey of learning and growing. Because your goal as a parent is to raise an independent, self-sufficient adult, you will prepare your child best by making yourself progressively unnecessary. In other words, you must allow your child to separate from you, little by little, until he is capable of functioning on his own.

Many times, children who are failing or doing poorly in school are proving their separateness. For underachievers, this is the only way to control their situation and satisfy their need for personal power. Parents and teachers who allow separateness usually observe that the children are more manageable because they have no need to misbehave.

Parents can foster this need for increased separation by giving children the power and freedom to learn responsibility. What is important is knowing what levels of power are appropriate for children at their different stages of development. Seek ways to make yourself progressively unnecessary.

Kids who are given power at an early age do not rebel as much when they are adolescents.

On Bullies

Bullying is usually a defensive tactic. Bullies are trying to be something and someone they are not. Why? Because they feel inadequate and want to hide themselves. They also do this to try and value themselves. Boys will gang up with other boys for support. So will girls. Then the gang will zero in on someone they perceive as weaker.

We have to teach our children a healthy self-concept so they can use it to "check" the bully and walk away. Cooperative learning groups can teach its members the responses that work in dealing with a bully. The child can then put the bully in situations where that bully can much easier gain the respect of others through acceptable behavior, not bullying.

Cooperative learning groups are great for shy kids, too. There they can get their strengths recognized and learn better responses to the demands of bullies and others.

About Report Cards

Report cards don't really give the parent or child an objective measure of learning by the child. They are more an informative, subjective evaluation for the parent given by the teacher of their own teaching effectiveness (W. Edwards Deming). Report cards represent extrinsic, rather than intrinsic, motivation.

About Parent/Teacher Conferences

In parent teacher conferences, parents can benefit by asking three questions. Is my child making progress? Does my child seem to feel good about being in school? How does my child get along with other kids?

Freedom to Be Responsible

Personal responsibility is the hallmark of self-esteem. You encourage responsible behavior when you reward your child with increased freedom. If the child is not ever given freedom, he will never learn to handle it. Then when age gives him freedom, he will literally go wild, unable to adjust to the new condition. Parents need to recognize and reward responsibility with freedom.

To illustrate, I remember a rule at our house: the children could play at any house in the neighborhood, but I had to know where they were. So, if my daughter was going to leave Sally's house to go play at Becky's, she had to come tell me first.

One evening in particular, just before dinner, my daughter, Camilla, came to me and said she was switching houses. It would have been very easy for me to say, "No, it's almost dinner time, come home now." But she had observed the rule and behaved in a responsible manner. So, I gave her the reward of freedom. I said, "Oh, great! You're very responsible to come tell me like we agreed. Run and go have fun." I held up dinner for 15 minutes. It was none the worse for the wait. My daughter learned a bit about growing up and was happy with her reward.

Different stages of development called for different levels of freedom. If your teen wants to stay out until 1:00 AM, you may allow it, as long as he phones you at midnight to let you know he's OK. If he abides by the rule, you can reward him another time by letting him try 12:30 or 1:00 AM. Even a child of three or four can learn responsibility. When you reward the child with freedom, the child feels good about himself, is inwardly motivated, and tries even harder.

Freedom to Fail

Children need to be given freedom to fail, as well. In order to know how far you can go, you must go beyond your capabilities and fail. It is the only way to discover your limits. You need to teach your child to chance it once in a while.

Training wheels are a really good example. Lots of kids use training wheels on their bikes. Learning to do without training wheels has a lot to do with desire, motivation, peer pressure, and basic motor development.

Ben was very motivated to do without his training wheels. I knew in my heart he just wasn't skilled enough, but I told him we will take the training wheels off whenever he feels ready. Sometimes it is hard to know when you are ready. I knew that if Ben found he didn't like riding without training wheels, we would just put them back on.

I watched Ben struggle for a day or two without the training wheels, and just bit my tongue. Eventually he came to me and said, "Mom, I don't think I'm ready to go without those training wheels yet." I said, "No problem." Then I put the wheels back on.

By giving Ben the freedom to make the decision, and thereby the freedom to fail, he felt good about himself, and the next time we took off the training wheels, he really was ready to ride that bike like a breeze.

Appropriate Power

The question isn't whether to give your child power or not. Children must be given power to grow, mature, and learn to solve problems. The real question is the appropriateness of power you give to your child. The appropriate power you give should be determined by his age, intelligence, degree of maturity, and his current developmental stage.

Asking your child to choose between two restaurants is OK. Requiring your child to select one of two nursery schools is unfair and hurries your child to grow up. Anytime you ask a child to understand beyond the limits of their understanding, or to decide beyond their capacity to make decisions, you are guilty of hurrying your child. Such requirements overtax a child's energy reserves and are usually demanded to make life easier for the parent, not the child.

For example, how many times did we take our tired child to one more store, or squish one more thing into the family schedule for our convenience? This overtaxes the child physically. The same is true of overtaxing his mental capacity by demanding he accept power or make decisions beyond his level of development just to alleviate your parental burden.

Much of your success as a parent will depend upon your awareness and understanding of the various developmental stages your child goes through. Knowing his age and readiness ability will help you assign only appropriate power to your child. Check your library or bookstore for one of the many good books available on ages and stages of child development. I have listed some sources at the end of this book.

The "Why Not Theory"

In 1921, George Bernard Shaw wrote his play, *Back to Methuselah*. In it, the Serpent is speaking to Eve in the Garden of Eden: "I hear you say "Why? Always "Why?" You see things; and you say,

"Why?" But I dream things that never were; and I say, "Why not?"

From these words, I have derived my "Why Not Theory."

Power struggles with your children are no fun. The "Why Not Theory" helps you see many situations you think are important, but that are really not such a big deal. "Why not" eliminates power struggles that often accompany little things.

Ben had a Swensen's birthday certificate for ice cream. The certificate entitled him to the sundae of his choice. Ben handed the waitress his certificate and ordered a bubble gum ice cream sundae with blueberry sauce.

The waitress stood motionless and looked at us, obviously waiting for us to say he couldn't have such an awful sundae. We exercised the "Why Not Theory" and said nothing. The waitress brought the sundae and Ben ate almost all of it. Why not? Where was the harm?

Camilla wanted to bake a cake, but we had only one egg. I called our neighbor, Sheila, but she was not at home. We decided to bake the cake anyway. Why not? It didn't taste that bad, but we had to glue it together with frosting. We learned a lot and it was cheaper than any toy!

Pioneer women before us walked westward with wagon trains to California and Oregon. We felt a small part of that in 1986 when we participated in "Hands Across America." Why not?

You can use "why not" at home, too. If your daughter wants to move her bed across the room, why not? If there's an important reason why she shouldn't, then fine. But if not, why not?

Camilla's bedroom needed repainting. We told her she could paint it any way she wanted, and we would help. She chose the paint and a two-tone design of her own, not a design we would have used. Why not?

Giving your child power over little things will fill their needs and you can retain power for yourself on larger issues.

Suppose your child asks to cross the street to see if a friend can come out and play. If you have seen the friend leave in the car a few minutes prior, you could say, "No, he left with his mother." But think. Crossing the street, ringing the doorbell, discovering the friend is not home, and coming back to tell you could keep the child busy for 15 minutes. And your child gains the power of finding out for himself. So, why not?

CHAPTER 4:
WHEN PROBLEMS ARISE, IMPROVISE!

Be Flexible

You and your child will both flourish if the atmosphere in your home is flexible. As they say in business, "We have just one inflexible rule, be flexible!"

Have you ever seen the limber pines on the mountain tops of Utah? They are the only trees able to take the winds and the snow. The branches are so flexible you can tie them in a knot. Moreover, when you untie the knot, the branches spring back to their original position!

Flexibility in your family is crucial, and so is springing back. So, when you are ready to leave on a picnic and have the car totally packed and the baby messes his diaper, you just stop and change his pants. Then, you spring back and still feel good about going on your outing, instead of whining, "Now it's too late and really won't be worth it."

Or perhaps it's your son's job to do the dinner dishes, but tonight he really wants to practice his trombone for the school recital tomorrow. If you're flexible, you'll agree practicing is important and let him trade chores with his sister.

When the climate in your house is flexible, your children learn that what they're doing can be as important as what you are doing or what the family is doing. This emphasizes their place as a valued member of the family.

Watch Me

Because you will encounter so many little problems in your daily adult life, the way you handle them will be noticed and modeled by your kids. Your children need to see you deal with problems, and you need to remember they are watching and learning.

When you're trying to solve a problem, it helps to state the problem out loud. "Gee, the car won't start. Well, this is the hassle because I wanted to go shopping. I guess we'll have to call a repair shot first and see if they can figure out what's wrong."

By avoiding comments like, "Oh dear, this is terrible. Now we will never get anywhere," your child won't get the idea it's the end of the world.

After you have solved a problem, remember to go back and share how good you feel about it with your child. Children will model positive self-talk, so do your best to build yourself up as you are working on a problem. "You know, fixing the car was a pain, but I feel good because we found out what the problem was and got it fixed. Now we can go shopping and we don't have to worry about the car starting."

Show your children that some problems can be solved right away, and others take time. Let your child know there are resources available to help solve the problems of daily life, and that it's always OK to ask for help. The most important thing, next to knowing the answer, is knowing where to find help!

Admit Mistakes

As your children watch the way you handle daily problems, you can earn respect from them if you freely admit your mistakes. Everyone knows children make a lot of mistakes, but how many kids know their parents do? When Mom and Dad admit to a goof up, it helps the child to understand that everyone is human.

Marilyn was in one of my parenting classes and truly thought she was a bad problem solver. She felt she let every little problem wipe her out, but she committed to trying some of the problem-solving techniques we discussed in class. The next week, she came back with a great success story.

It seems the household was in the usual morning uproar as everyone prepared for work and school. Marilyn's daughter was told to take out the trash, and as she lifted the bag, it burst, covering her with leftover spaghetti and a variety of other yucky stuff. It was time to leave in the carpool, and the entire family stood motionless, looking at the daughter covered in spaghetti. Marilyn took a deep breath and said, "Well, next time I'll buy stronger trash bags!" Immediately, the entire family was at ease, and the children saw their mother admit a mistake, then proceed to deal positively with the problem. It was a very effective lesson for the kids, and Marilyn felt great about herself in the process!

The Smooth Handle

Thomas Jefferson advises us to, "Take life by the smooth handle." If you can follow his advice, you will find you save yourself and your children lots of headaches.

What does it mean to take the smooth handle? Simply stated — when life presents a situation, look for the easiest, least stressful way out.

For example, the druggist once sent Ben some allergy medicine in liquid form. Ben hates to take liquid medicine. We could have struggled with this, but instead I chose the smooth handle. We took the liquid medicine back and exchanged it for pill form. Ben was happy and felt I was sensitive to his needs. I was happy because he took his medicine without complaint.

When you're dealing with the "everydays," remember these time-tested sayings, "If it ain't broke don't fix it." "This too shall pass." "There's more than one way to skin a cat." And "Take life by the smooth handle." The reason these words of wisdom have stuck around so long is because they have a great deal of merit!

When your child has a problem, it's very difficult to remember your job is to guide. To truly help your child learn to solve problems, though, you must refrain from jumping in and handling the problem for her. If you do, she will feel that you see her as incapable and, as a result, she will begin to doubt herself.

A young mother I knew was sick with the flu and spent the day laying on the couch as her five-year-old played. It was a beautiful snowy day and eventually the child got antsy and wanted to go outside. Obviously, the mother could not go outside, so they discussed the situation and agreed the little girl could go out if she played right in front of the window so her mother could look out and check on her.

The girl bundled up, went outside, and built a little snowman. She was so excited that she ran inside and begged her mother to come see the snowman. Again, her mother explained why she could not go out. In the face of an imminent tantrum, she assumed the role of a guide to help solve the problem.

The mother said, "You want me to see the snowman, and I'd like to see the snowman, but I can't go outside. What do you think we can do about this?" After a series of provocative questions, the child suggested she could take the Polaroid camera outside and bring back a picture for her mother. A perfect solution! And one that the child felt good about because she came up with it herself. Chalk up another one for increasing self-esteem!

Life is Daily

You are raising a child (or children) from birth to adulthood. You will have problems and so will the children. To teach your children problem solving, you must learn to look at problems as challenges to be solved, rather than some wild neurotic monsters out to get you.

Honestly, what are the problems you deal with the most? If you're in the majority, you deal with problems of daily life, like the dishwasher broke, the cleaners lost your sweater, there's nothing defrosted for dinner, or it's raining, and the kids are bored. Woe is you!

To feel good about yourself, look at daily problems as lessons to solve and make you stronger. There's no need to be scared, because you're not facing monsters!

Anyway

This is a favorite handout, written by Dr. Kent M. Keith in 1968, that I have used in all of my classes. (See his *YouTube* videos.)

The Paradoxical Commandments

People are illogical, unreasonable, and self-centered.
Love them anyway.

If you do good, people will accuse you of selfish ulterior motives.
Do good anyway.

If you are successful, you will win false friends and true enemies.
Succeed anyway.

The good you do today will be forgotten tomorrow.
Do good anyway.

Honesty and frankness make you vulnerable.
Be honest and frank anyway.

The biggest men and women with the biggest ideas can be shot down by the smallest men and women with the smallest minds.
Think big anyway.

People favor underdogs but follow only top dogs.
Fight for a few underdogs anyway.

What you spend years building may be destroyed overnight.
Build anyway.

People really need help but may attack you if you do help them.
Help people anyway.

Give the world the best you have and you'll get kicked in the teeth.
Give the world the best you have anyway.

CHAPTER 5:
HOW IS THE CLIMATE?

No Success? Check the Climate

Climate is how it feels to live in your home or to be in your classroom. If your child is not experiencing success, check the climate at home and school. Ask, "How does it feel to live in your house?" "How does it feel to be in your first-grade classroom?"

The climate, or environment, you provide for your child will play a major part in the development of his self-esteem. If your child is not meeting with success on a regular basis, check the climate of his environment and you will likely spot the trouble.

Children need an encouraging, supportive climate both at home and at school, but it is the family environment that is most instrumental in building self-esteem and teaching communication skills.

An encouraging climate is generous with the words "imagination" and "wonderful." Albert Einstein said, "Imagination is more important than knowledge, for knowledge is limited, while imagination embraces the entire world."

Dreaming

Children understand imagination and day-dreaming. Everyone has a dream they are not meeting, something they are working toward. If you are meeting all your dreams, set your dreams higher with realistic signposts along the way. Hard work and good luck go together. Let your children know some of your dreams and let them see the work you do to realize them.

Stay In Touch

Mother Teresa said, "Loneliness is a bigger problem than poverty in today's world." In some families I've dealt with, parents tell me they felt out of touch with their kids before the children reached five or six years old!

For your child's healthy development as well as your own happiness, work at keeping in touch with your family. How? Begin by recognizing two important aspects of the family, the *doing* and the *being*. Balance between them is important in families.

Doing and Being

You learn personal humaneness and personal dignity being in a family. You learn you have potential. You know there is something there in you; you just know it. You can find who you really are in your family easier than you can anywhere else.

The doing and the being of a family are different, but equally important, aspects of staying in touch. The doing of your family includes the shopping, eating, vacationing, arguing, and so on. The doing is important because it involves the "everydays." While it doesn't sound very romantic, we often find ourselves just cleaning the toilet or mowing the grass.

The being of your family is more intangible. It's the "I know you, and know what you care about, and you know me. You know what is going on in my head and my heart." Families who stay in touch with good family communication nurture the being aspect of the family by making sure all the members feel valued. An important way to do this is to give all members of the family—adults and children alike—some focused attention.

We want to share ourselveswith our children. One way is to share the things we had fun doing while growing up.

As a child, we had a chinaberry tree in our yard, and it was a neat tree. We cooked berries from it, and we shot slingshots with them. I sat in our chinaberry tree. There was a limb on the tree for a horse, so I rode the chinaberry tree. Part of being a child is having ritual things to enjoy and play.

Our children need to know what we did and how we felt when we were children. Take dating. We can really help them if we share how we dated, how awkward we felt, how our first kiss felt, or how we felt when given our first corsage. I need to share such things to show them the way I grew up and learned the tool called myself. I need to share that I craved peppermint ice cream when I was pregnant with you. These are being things.

The Japanese have a wonderful word, *muga*. It means total present moment awareness. Focused attention is an extremely powerful tool for making your child feel valued and for keeping in touch. The beauty of focused attention is that it doesn't have to take a long time and it can even help you manage your time better.

Suppose your daughter comes home with all of her Valentines and spends 30 minutes following you around the kitchen trying to show them to you while you struggle to fix dinner. Instead, you could say, "I'm going to take 10 minutes right now and sit down with you to look at your Valentines. Dinner can wait." Ten minutes of your total attention is heaven for the child, and after the ten minutes of sharing time, you can get back to your dinner without interruption. Giving your child your total attention, even if just for a very short while, will increase her self-esteem, build your relationship, and foster a climate for open communication.

Stay in touch at home. With good family communications, members feel valued. Build relationships by sharing feelings, by physical closeness, by hugging and touching appropriate for the situation. Practice saying, "I feel . . ." instead of saying, "You feel . . ." This kind of focused attention is one of the greatest forces for change in your toolbox.

Parents are leaders and guides, not family bosses. Your goal is to help create independent adults out of your children. To do this, give each child both freedom and responsibility. They need that power to learn and solve problems.

Preparing for Change

Be flexible when problems arise and spring back. Learn to stretch your thinking. There is more than one way to make iced tea (like sun tea).

Remember that children live in the present, so try to see the world through their eyes. Take the time to share their magic moments with them, and yours, too.

Your job is to prepare your children for change and to welcome it, so plan activities where the child can succeed. Frequent successes will build a "cushion of success" for the failures to come.

Playboy in High School

In high school, some boys were sitting in the front row of English class opening up *Playboy* magazine. All the kids in the back row could see the centerfold. My husband and I were talking about that and laughing about it, and he said, "You know, keep it cool, keep it shockproof. That's not the end of the world. That is adolescence." Then he said, "Oh, have they got the new *Playboy* yet without the staple in the navel? It's much easier to look at." We laughed, because now we could talk about it.

Acting like one thing is happening while another thing is happening is very dangerous to children. To assume just because you don't like *Playboy*, that it's not happening, confuses children, because it is happening. They're holding up *Playboy* in school; they're showing *Playboy* to the back row. If you say, "That's awful, that isn't real, and that's not happening," then the child or the adolescent says, "Something is wrong here, this is real, this is happening."

Keeping our cool as parents is extremely important. The less we get uptight about such things, the more our children are able to decide what they really want to be doing in school, or not be doing. If we are too heavy handed, the adolescent becomes locked into resistance and will never be able to learn. I think the teacher will have to say to kids of this age, "You may either look at *Playboy* or you may learn English. If you look at *Playboy*, you will fail. You will not get an A out of this class if that's what you are going to put your time on."

A teacher has a real responsibility to follow through, just as a parent has a responsibility to follow through. The teacher says, "You get a choice. You want to look at *Playboy*? That's fine, but I will grade in these ways and these things will happen in my class. If you choose not to do these things, you will fail. You may not graduate from high school. You may not like it, but that's the way it is." These are the strong logical consequences of high school.

Doing

Don't forget to let your child do what he is able to do. I remember that *Grabbitz* was a family game we liked to play because you could have several levels of kids playing and still have fun. We forgot that Ben was old enough to keep score. We usually either kept score or gave it to his older sister. One night I said, "Ben, you can keep score." His eyes lit up so big.

Make sure you don't forget that the younger child is growing and changing and starting to do a lot of things that the older siblings can do, but you're so used to having them do it that you don't ask the younger child. The younger child remains a baby. If you are aware of their growth, a younger child can answer the phone, go get an egg, butter his bread, and keep score in a game. This will help the whole family. The family will begin to respect the younger child, too.

But no one has to keep anyone a baby. Many times, we keep the child a baby by forgetting what they can do, by not letting them practice it, and then by not letting them grow up and do bigger things. Bigger is getting the loaf of bread. Bigger is ready to mow the lawn or work with tools in the workshop.

Everybody needs to be needed, but we have to be careful that we don't keep people locked into being needed, or keep them powerless, just to make ourselves feel good.

Listening

We have to be careful with our listening. My daughter has told me so many times, "Mother, you're hearing, but you're not listening!" Listening means focusing on that person and hearing just exactly what they have to say, so you can feed it back to them. It's such a difficult art to really hear what someone says, to listen and feed it back, and not give any judgments.

Kids trick us. They trick us verbally. As they get bigger, they are more verbal and we assume that everything they say, they understand. This is not true. We need to listen carefully and know when they are tricking us verbally. We think they are grown up, and then they say something to remind us they are kids.

A sophomore in high school, a sophisticated girl who had so much knowledge and so much verbalness, was watching *Gone with the Wind* with her mother. She asked, "Who in the world won this war anyway?" We assume that they know the whole story of the American Civil War after watching *Gone with the Wind*.

Another girl in high school thought that the Pope was Jewish because he wore one of those little round hats. How she put things together makes perfect sense. Why is the Pope not Jewish? He wears a little Jewish hat.

One of my son's friends in 5th grade is also ten years old. They like to get together and scheme. The friend called me on the phone before my son arrived home and said that they had already talked with "my dad." Instead of saying "your husband," he said, "We've already talked with your dad, and he says it's OK with you that we can play together."

Listening very carefully to these kinds of things shows us that children don't always have the knowledge and the wisdom that we think they have underneath their verbalness. At ten years old, he's still calling my husband, "my dad." We see and hear that a lot with younger children, but not so much with ten-year-olds. Yes, this child is ten and he's calling my husband "my dad." He's very bright and very verbal and very much a boy.

One of my fourth-grade teacher friends says that she sees this all the time. The boys are so big and so macho in the schoolroom. They are zipping around being really cool and saying they went to Cahokia Mounds for a field trip. But there were some bees there and they totally lost it. They were running around like little babies, scared of the bees, and squealing and squeaking and jumping all over everywhere. These fourth graders are so cool in their schoolroom. They fool us again and again because we don't get under their verbalness.

Keep the Door Open

Here's another story about children appearing older than they are.

Some boys were playing in the block area, and they had their cars set up, their bridge set up, and their road set up. They seemed mature. They knew everybody's name and they knew who was doing what. Then one of the four-year-old boys got bumped. When he got bumped, his body became a baby again. He started to cry. He went back to the teacher and the teacher nurtured him. She kept the door open. She didn't say, "You're acting like a baby, you shouldn't come crying, you were big and playing with all those cars and now look at what you're doing." She nurtured him. Then she said, "I think your friends need you again."

As we see our children grow up, it's important that we keep the door open. We don't say, "You're a baby to cry, you're a big boy now." You open the door, you let them come, you nurture them, but you don't hold on to them. You move them back to their friends. "I think your friends need you. I think you need to go on building." The door must always be opened for them to go back and forth from security to safety, then on to something new. When a child moves from security and safety to confidence, that's growth.

Pool Story

One of my friends at the pool was a gifted swimmer. He was four and could dive off the board and swim like the big kids. He was very good at swimming. He loved to swim and dive in the deep end. Then we would look around and wonder where he went. He went back to the baby pool. He could not maintain the big pool the whole time. He had to go back to security. We all move from confidence to security.

When we are at the pool in the summer, our husbands may think we're eating bonbons and tanning, but we're going from one pool to the other pool when the child wants to have the challenge and also needs security. We always want to keep the door open and not make them feel bad about coming back to the baby pool, or about coming back and sitting on the teacher's lap when they get hurt playing with blocks.

The door must always be open for our children to feel good about themselves. They must always know the door is open to move from security to confidence. Two steps forward and one step back. In and out, with an open door that says, "It's OK," instead of a closed door that says, 'You're a crybaby, we don't want you to come back anymore, you've been climbing the ladder for six months, and now you can't climb it."

We are watching a problem-solving process when the child has been doing something, then, all of a sudden, slides back to security. Now we can say, "What's your plan? Could you take two steps down? Which foot do you want to use?" Give them the problem-solving technique to move to security, rather than disabling them and saying, "I'll do it for you, I'll lift you all the way down."

A lot of children, when they have a security confidence issue, have played down in the basement for six months by themselves with their toys with no problem. All of a sudden, they don't want to go downstairs and play. They want to bring their toys upstairs, or they want to hold your hand on the steps after they have been going up and down by themselves. Or they have been going by themselves into the school classroom, and all of a sudden, they want you to go with them. The door must stay open for children to feel good about themselves. Tell them, "It's OK to move from security to confidence."

All this goes back to adultness, about being separate again. After all, the feelings of being a separate self are what a child's stubbornness is all about. It is not defiance about who's the boss. It is his or her new feeling of separateness, and that is OK. We have to let our children feel OK about their separateness and their new and emerging selves.

Remember, the people who were good for us when we were children, were people who made us feel good, not bad, about our emerging separateness and we are glad. We parents have to do a lot of practicing separateness. We have to allow ourselves, I think, to mourn a little and say, "Gee, they don't need me as much as they used to, and my mourning a little bit about that is OK." Allow yourself that.

Ritual is Important

I once read that a wrinkled brain is supposedly better than a smooth brain. So, every morning when I dropped Ben off at school, I said, "Stretch and grow and wrinkle that brain today, Ben."

One day I didn't say it, and Ben said, "Hey, Mom, say that thing about the wrinkle." I didn't even think he cared that much, but he did. I realized it was our ritual. Ritual is important to children. It helps them realize you are there for them, no matter what. You say or do the same thing every day, whether the child has been a problem or not. When Ben requested "wrinkle and stretch," I realized it was a ritual, a part of my day and a part of his. This phrase bound us to one another and helped us keep in touch as he grew up. We exchange rituals every day, so look for yours in your own life.

My father was very good at staying in touch. He used to give me a little salute when I was young, and I saluted back. He saluted and I saluted. When I was a teenager, he continued saluting, but I thought it was silly, and I felt sorry for him. So, I'd do a little bitty tiny salute to acknowledge his presence, but I'd tell him how he was embarrassing me. I'd tell him he was silly, but he never quit doing his salute. I never knew when he'd peek around the corner and give me a salute.

My father knew the secret about rituals and keeping in touch. The secret is this. Do it even when your kids don't do it back. As the parent, establish rituals with your children. And do them, do them, do them, and do them, without expecting any appreciation or feedback in return because children know. Just believe in the importance of what you're doing. Stay in touch.

All Feelings Count

Humans are capable of experiencing six major feelings: anger, pain, embarrassment, fear, love, and happiness. Most people will agree that feelings are important and that all feelings are legitimate, but many of us were raised to believe negative feelings are bad and should not be felt. Feelings help us stay in touch.

I contend that feelings are energy, and energy flows. Feelings have to go somewhere, regardless of their positive or negative qualities. In households with an open climate, families talk about feelings, and this sharing strengthens their relationships.

Talking about feelings reduces tension and makes the feelings easier to deal with. When people express their feelings, they usually act more wisely. When a child is not allowed to express negative feelings in words, the most likely result is antisocial behavior, anxiety, depression, or perhaps them all.

Always acknowledge your child's expression of feelings. All feelings must be respected. This is not to say you should let your child manipulate you, but by acknowledging his feelings, he will know you care. For example, if your daughter screams, "I hate taking a bath," she still must bathe, but you don't have to negate her feelings. You can say, "Is it because you want to keep playing this game? We can take a speedy bath." Or you can say, "Baths are the pits, huh? But we all have to take baths. Would you like to take yours before your TV program, or after?"

Your feelings as a parent are important to acknowledge, too. Your child needs to stay in touch with you as much as you want to keep in touch with him. So be honest with your children about your feelings. Don't say one thing when you're feeling another. You will not fool the kids. That will make them distrust their own feelings as bad energy.

It is not what we say but how we feel that is most important.

Practice "I-Talk"

One last suggestion I have to help your family's communication is to practice speaking to your children with "I-Talk."

"I-Talk" means starting your statements with the word I instead of You. What this will do is help you to separate your child from his behavior, and help your child understand the consequences of his actions.

Suppose you are talking to a business associate on the phone and the kids are running through the house screaming. Your first inclination may be to scream louder and say, "Would you kids cool it? You're entirely too rowdy and you're downright rude!" The real message to your children is that they are rowdy and downright rude, in other words, bad kids.

What if you said instead, "I am having trouble talking on the phone with all this noise." The message to the children is not a personal attack. If your family is one that has established a climate of respect for all members, you're very likely to get the results you're looking for with "I-Talk." Remember this distinguishable difference, "YOU" leads to criticism and accusations, while "I" leads to an undeniable expression of feelings.

The Problem with Praise

There is a distinct difference between praise and encouragement. Praise goes only one way, from you to the child. Encouragement proliferates to all who hear it.

You, an adult, would not say to Babe Ruth, "You are a great player and doing a fine job." You would not dare to judge Babe Ruth. That would be arrogant and in bad taste. However, you might easily say, "Thank you, Mr. Ruth. Your baseball playing has brought me great joy and enriched my life." Likewise, children deserve the same. They also need appreciation, and do not deserve criticism or comparison.

Encouragement is addictive to the child, and it grows them roots of courage.

It is extremely difficult to make parents understand the danger of praising a child, especially when the parents are striving to create a nurturing climate and open communication. But the danger exists, and you really need to try to understand the difference between praise and encouragement.

Praise is like a drug. It makes a child happy at the time, but it trains him to always look to others for approval. Praise is not always verbal, either.

Consider how many children are offered bribes to make good grades. Recognition of this type is only superficial.

Encouragement, on the other hand, separates the deed from the doer, and allows the child to know internally he is OK. The trick to using encouragement, instead of praise, is to state what you see.

One summer, I worked as a tutor, and one of my students was a young girl who had problems writing reports. We worked on reports all summer and I taught her ways to do research, how to use index cards, and what type of questions to ask herself, etc. Toward the end of the summer, I was working in the garden when the girl and her mother pulled up in my driveway. She had come to show me a report she was particularly proud of, and the report was good. But I wanted to use just the right words to tell her what I thought. The words came. I said, "You don't need me anymore." Her shining eyes told me it was the perfect response that meant so much more than a simple "good paper." Give your child responses and reports that strengthen, so she will know she is strong enough to do things on her own.

When your Little Leaguer hits a home run and you say, "Gosh you're great! You're the best hitter! You're terrific!" he will certainly feel good for the moment. But what happens the next time he bats and doesn't hit a home run? He may tell himself, "I'm bad, I'm the worst hitter, I'm no good anymore."

The solution is easy to say and harder to do. If you state what you see, good or bad, the evaluation of the event will be left to the child himself. Instead of praise like, "You're the best ball player," use encouraging words like "Your home run went far. I sure enjoyed seeing you run those bases!" This will make your child feel just as good about himself as praise will.

Since encouragement separates the deed from the doer, the child does not associate the particular accomplishment with the very essence of his being as a worthy person, and subsequent failure is less likely to harm his self-image.

Encouraging phrases can be used to demonstrate acceptance ("I like the way you . . ."), show confidence ("I know you can . . ."), extend appreciation ("Thanks, that was thoughtful of you to . . ."), and acknowledge effort, as in ("I see you are improving in . . .").

So, if you see a home run, acknowledge the home run. If a poem is nice, say you enjoyed reading it. If you're given a picture, comment on the pretty colors. If you state what you see and leave the child to evaluate himself, you will encourage independence, an adult trait you are advancing.

Here is what I learned from Haim Ginott's writing on *The Perils of Praise*.

> *The single most important rule is that praise deal only with children's efforts and accomplishments, not with their character and personality.*

CHAPTER 6:
TAKE ROOT AND GROW

Moving From Security to Confidence

When listening to your child, understand and recognize their growing self. Don't get discouraged when your child slides back. For example: wanting a bottle again when the new baby arrives. Replace the child's fears by your reassuring love. Avoid hurrying the child. Just as we don't buy clothes for them that several sizes too big, we shouldn't expect behaviors several sizes too big.

On the other hand, when we expect too little of children, we rob them of their opportunity to contribute. We do want to have expectations. No expectations mean, "Hey, my child can't contribute anything." We want challenge that is constructive, not debilitating like a sieve.

I think one of the hardest things about parenting is when we act like a sieve, letting through what we think a child can handle and holding back what we think they can't. We want to say, "Yes, he can handle that. We will let it through. Or, oops, that's too much, we won't let it through." The adult is responsible for the sieve. So many parents ask me, "Well, how much?" You have to feel it and know it for your own child. Every child is different.

Enjoy Your Child as a Growing Person

Enjoy your child as a growing person, ready to mow the lawn or build something in the workshop.

Everybody needs to be needed, but we have to be careful that we don't keep people locked into being needed just to make ourselves feel good and hold somebody else powerless. People who need to be needed are not filling their pitcher in positive ways.

CHAPTER 7:
YOUR CURIOUSLY CREATIVE CHILD

The Creative Climate

Curiosity and growth are partners. A child's creativity thrives in a climate where creativity is truly and clearly valued. Process is more important than product! It is not important whether a child becomes an artist. What is important is teaching your child to live a life of wonder, appreciating beauty. Then they will develop genuine creativity.

I Wonder

Create a non-threatening atmosphere for wonder. Teach the child to observe. Ask the child what she wonders about. Provide toys that stimulate imagination. Provide lots of materials to work with. Avoid art materials that inhibit imagination and require playing adult stereotypes "one way." Dress up clothes provide rich opportunities. Give opportunities to create their own "tender little messes." Encourage all kinds of self-expression. Be tolerant of errors and help the child to use their mistakes. Remember children learn by doing. Remember knowing is not understanding.

It is important to listen to what the child wonders about. When he was nine, Ben asked me, "How do you know a tablespoon of butter when it is in a stick?"

Encouraging Creativity

I remember teaching a parenting class using flip sheets. Some mothers had dragged reluctant husbands to the course. The mothers already knew spelling was not my strong suit. A superior-sounding father pointed out that I had misspelled the word "they" as "thay." I saw he was right and agreed. Then I shared a quote with him attributed to Mark Twain, "I have no respect for a man who can spell a word only one way." The whole class roared and accepted me as is, as did he.

Parent Guidelines for Child Creativity

A child's play is his work. Play is learning by doing. They encounter life in structured and unstructured play. They process, learn, and give back in play.

Play is hard work, their work. Watching them play helps us parents learn what the child knows and what the child understands. Knowing is not the same as understanding. A child may be able to count to a hundred, yet not be able to fetch four napkins for the table.

Here are some ideas for enriching a child's creative capacity for play:

Create a non-threatening atmosphere.

Teach the child to observe.

Ask the child what he/she wonders about.

Provide toys that stimulate imagination.

**Provide a variety of materials
that can be manipulated.**

Avoid art materials that limit imagination.

**Keep in mind that the process
is more important than the product.**

**Encourage natural abilities and self-expression:
dancing, music, writing, etc.**

**Tolerate errors and show your child
how to learn from the gift of mistakes.**

Ask open ended questions.

CHAPTER 8:
DEVELOPING SOCIAL ABILITIES

Competition and Cooperation

Competition is valuable as a motivator only for those who believe they can win. However, those who think they have no chance of winning are not motivated by competition and are more likely to be discouraged, disillusioned, and not try.

Arthur Combs said this about competition succinctly, "When competition becomes too important, morality breaks down and any means becomes acceptable to achieve desired ends."

Sportsmanship and cooperation develop from numerous experiences in competition.

A Respect for Manners

We all see our children imitate us. They learn from us appropriate greetings and the acknowledgement of others. When they notice adults respecting each other and respecting children, they learn respect for everyone, including themselves.

There is something nice about hearing someone say your name. It validates your existence as a human being. Notice the waiter's name tag and use it when ordering. You will, invariably, get better service.

I was once on a committee for evaluating school teachers. The ones who said the names of children seemed to be more nurturing, especially when they get down on the child's eye level, pick them up, or stoop down. Parents and teachers seem much more human to the child at that level. A child explained it better, "I can't tell the teacher. Would you tell the Green Giant?"

Parents and teachers who know that a child can only learn when she is feeling valued and values herself don't respond in ways that make a child feel devalued. When a child is acting responsibly, give the child more freedom rather than more responsibility. When a child is acting responsibly, comment on what the child *is doing*. Describe what happened. "I appreciate you picking up your room while I was gone."

A Respect for Feelings

Human life and human feelings are more important than anything else. We often forget the miracle in each of our children and take it for granted when we are with them day after day. We prize them, but so often don't show that we do. Pick a day this week and show a family member you prize them.

It takes great wisdom to realize that all feelings are legitimate because we have often been taught that negative feelings are bad, should not be felt and we should be ashamed of them. Feelings have to go somewhere because feelings are energy. If they are released into the air by talking about them, the speaker feels better.

When a child cannot express feelings with words because they lack the vocabulary, they will likely engage in anti-social behavior, become anxious, seem depressed, or all of these. Listen carefully and help your child express what he feels.

Children really live in the present while parents often prepare ahead of time for what is to come in the future.

In order to help children, we must separate our own sense of self from the behavior of the child. When another child calls your child a dummy and stupid, it hurts your child's feelings, but when a teacher or parent says the same thing, the child assumes it to be true.

There will be problems in life, of course. But life is not so difficult if we know how to handle problems and feel great about solving them.

Nurturing parents are polite. When we are polite, it shows in the simplest way that we value and care about feelings. Politeness releases stress and helps people become sensitive to the condition of others.

Families accept change as an unavoidable part of being alive and use this to help make their families more nurturing. "You are changing. You are now able to whistle when you couldn't before. I notice how you are growing."

Children change from one stage of growth to another. They go from a stage of equilibrium to one of dis-equilibrium, then back to equilibrium again. And we adults also never stop changing. The world around us doesn't stand still.

In a sense, we are like a lobster. In order to fit in his shell as he grows bigger, the lobster periodically sheds his shell. During these times, he is naked and vulnerable and in terrible danger of being eaten by predators, yet he must risk all to keep growing. He must go with the water current of life instead of fighting upstream. There he notices the unbelievable beauty of the waterflow and the miracle of his unfolding, his precious possibility of renewal coming from inside.

The Essential Ingredient

Love is the essential ingredient in our growth. Love does take work. The work of love is communication. We have to share feelings to be close. This is a simple truth: to know a person, you must share feelings. You can share a house, food, sex, and still not feel close. But you can't share feelings and not feel close. To share feelings, you must be able to say your fears, angers, hurts, without adding "I told you so." When your child comes in and says, "I kicked so and so," listen with wisdom, listen with love, and not find fault. Love heals a lot of wounds.

Ben lost his shoe. Camilla told me later that she knew where the shoe was. She told me she knew she was wrong to say nothing. That was simple evidence confirming our good relationship.

If you want to break a bad habit, you must first become aware of it and how you usually act. I have to see how I do it before I can undo it.

One basic difficulty for parents occurs when their children are childish. Their immaturity is a powerful stimulus to respond in a childlike manner. The child acts as a magnet to draw the parent into their orbit of immaturity.

Are you able to separate the child from their behavior? Can you say, "I love you but not what you are doing."

Ben was in the second grade. When I picked him up from school, he said, "What are you doing here?" He was in a really bad mood and not sure about having me around. I felt he must be somehow embarrassed at my coming because he was always glad to see me. He just wanted to get out of school as fast as possible.

I made no assumptions, asked no questions, and said nothing. The next day I found out that he was upset because he had gotten in trouble during music class.

Making Ourselves Progressively Unnecessary

Children are always giving us clues. They usually know when they are ready for the next step, just as we know when we are ready. If we expect too little, we rob them of the opportunity to feel they have a contribution to make. If we expect too much, they never do it, producing low self-esteem and stress. "I can't do it!"

Ben was almost six. He wanted to do his homework on lined paper. He came over and said, "Have we got any of that lined paper? Can you get me some?" He was learning beginning sounds. I found the paper for him and said nothing more. The next day he said, "I like writing on that lined paper."

Camilla was taking violin in seventh grade. She came home crying, saying she was not playing well. I said, "What are you going to do?" She decided to ask her instructor for the name of an outside teacher.

We need to make ourselves progressively *unnecessary*. We have to teach children how to handle situations because we can't always be there to help. They don't feel helpless and afraid when they know they have options.

Be a Sieve, Not a Wall

Be a sieve, not a wall, giving them what they can handle slowly. The question is not should I give them the decision, but the appropriateness of the particular demand given their age, intelligence, and level of maturity. Asking a child to decide between two restaurants is OK. Requiring them to select one of two nursery schools to attend is unfair.

When we ask a child to understand beyond the limits of their understanding or decide beyond their capacity to make decisions, we overtax their energy reserves in order to make life easier for ourselves. This is the definition of hurrying the child.

The feelings of mastery over external events, that something can be done to remedy the situation or solve the problem, will protect children from depression. Show the child the unconsidered alternatives. It is a terribly wrong thing to assume that you, the parent, are totally responsible for your child's happiness. No one is responsible for another's happiness.

It's OK to Ask for Help

Do you ever feel the ocean is so big and my boat is so small? That boat of yours is not so small when it is attached to other boats. You — parent or child — have more courage when you have the support of others. It is OK to ask for help from peers, from those you trust who are wise.

Parent peers can step in, help you see from a new perspective, make that call for you. They are a source of comfort and insight. They can see if you are on the wrong track. They also provide needed humor in a bad situation, so it is less frightening and overwhelming, and so you don't take yourself too seriously. They can give you momentary escape with a coffee break or get you involved in something else. Of course, there will be problems; expecting there will be none is what gets us in trouble. Solving problems is a secret, personal triumph.

Camilla said she knows why the Muppet assistant to Dr. Bunsen Honeydew is called Beaker. She did a science experiment in school using beakers. This is one example of how children find personal meaning in life.

If the child is doing a good job and working hard on spelling or multiplication, reward him. Say, "You worked hard today, let's stop early now." The child will want to come back the next day feeling capable of new learning.

Life has many problems, large and small, and it is our reactions to them that are important. When we overreact, we tend to give the child the impression it is the end of the work. If we always make a big deal of spilled milk just like wrecking the car, we are unintentionally teaching that both are equally important to us.

In the seventh grade, Camilla got on the wrong bus, but just laughed about it. Another time she dropped her textbook and smiled about it. I said, "See how you've changed? Remember when you could not laugh about the same things? I believe in you. Now go believe in yourself."

There are two aspects of parenthood: one is challenging and creative—the growth part—and the other is chores and maintenance—the no growth part.

Benjamin Franklin said, "If man could have half his wishes, he would double his troubles." Small wonder someone told him to go fly a kite! Actions bring responsibility. There seems to be one enduring fact about bringing up small children: there is no rest. If you have no husband, or if you have hostility toward your husband who is never around to take his share of chores, then raising a child becomes doubly hard.

Through sports, children learn competence, self-assurance, and teamwork. But this is by no means true for all who participate. Structuring sports and games according to adult rules negates their value as playtime. At all levels of development, children need the opportunity to play for play's sake. Why? Because play is nature's way of dealing with stress for children as well as adults. Supposedly, man invented sports to enhance his life, but that purpose is often ignored today. When a Little Leaguer comes down with an anxiety attack over his performance, where has the joy of the game gone?

How can I help my child right now, not in the distant future, or far off Utopia, but right now? Just do the best you can with the knowledge you have at the time. As we know more, we broaden our knowledge, and can do more. Do what you can to help when you can.

Our sins as teachers and parents are many. But it is OK, OK, OK to be human and focus on what we can do to make things a little better, rather than having to find the ultimate solution.

Once again, remember these words. "Take life by the smooth handle," said Thomas Jefferson. "Don't fix things that aren't broken." And perhaps the most useful words of all, "This too shall pass."

Growth is a relinquishing and a receiving. We cut out the underbrush for the plants to grow. To grow as humans, we must change, give up, and learn anew. We renew in between. Children give up what doesn't help them anymore. They give up the breast for the bottle. They give up crawling for walking. Children naturally want what they want when they want it. With free play comes laughter. Laughter is our inner giggling made public.

Get the help you need. When a person is drowning, it is not the time to ask if they read the NO SWIMMING sign. It is OK to ask for help. Strong people ask for help. They say, "I can choose my own way even when I feel helpless."

Here are some ways we exert active control in a situation. We use choice and initiative. We are not static beings incapable of action. We are verbs, not nouns.

CHAPTER 9:
IT'S CHILD'S PLAY

A Child's Play is Their Work

Children encounter life in their play. Play is their hard work.

Children take the skills and information they learn and give it back through play. Watching your child at play will let you know what the child really understands.

Adults must balance the child's time between structured play (soccer, ballet lessons, etc.) and free play (wading in the creek, flashlight tag, etc.). Free play is different for different children.

Problems arise when parents and teachers ignore the need for play. Consider the many constructive purposes of play:

- **It is vital for the total development of a child**

- **It is a time to practice being myself without competition**

- **It helps children build relationships and social skills while they relate to** one another and negotiate their fantasies

- It teaches persistence and patience

- It adds meaning to experiences

- It is an antidote to hurrying and gives time to grow

- It teaches that you can have facts with no thinking, but you must have facts to have thinking

- It allows children to be initiators and organizers of self-directed activities such as rolling a ball to another, or playing in the creek

- It encourages joy and fun, the universal emotions of self-esteem

- It shows children they can grow and be OK

- It allows children a vehicle for thoughts and feelings that lead to understanding and communication

- It helps children socialize with other people

- It helps children learn to be alone without being lonely

- It helps children to master hobbies from novice to expert

- **It teaches children control over their world**

- **It utilizes curiosity in order to learn, and**

- **It is a great opportunity to practice using imagination through make believe play**

Play is an extremely complex phenomenon, not yet completely understood. It gives personal meaning to experience. With no personal meaning, there is no change in behavior.

Play develops imagination and is the root of all creativity. Play gives opportunities for children to turn boxes into spaceships and paper into hats. The simplest materials often provide the deepest meaning.

"Play is the highest expression of human development in childhood, for it alone is the free expression of what is in a child's soul," said Friedrich Froebel, the founder of kindergarten.

Child and Parent Choices

Being a child today is very complicated because of so many choices. A lot of choices call for a higher level of thinking and children need our guidance in making choices.

Helping a child today is also complicated by wading through the maze of so many choices.

Play: Perhaps the Best Teacher You Ever Had[1]

> *Janet decides that Sandra will be the mommy, she will be the daddy, and Joey will be the baby. Ben, who recently went to a play, has made a stage and is putting on a puppet show for the fourth day in a row. Janice stamps envelopes and writes letters just like her mommy does at work. Tommy just plays and does nothing. Billy makes a garage, but it is so tall that Chris helps him make a ramp for the cars. Todd and Greg enjoy Halloween by creating their own haunted house.*

These children have been given the time to explore their world through play. Problems come when adults ignore the need for play and overscheduled children both at home and school. In recent years both teachers and parents have expressed concerns about problems they see in

[1] by Carolyn Harden in *Growing Times* (©1985).

today's children. Play serves many purposes and can eliminate some of the concerns parents and teachers have.

Difficulty in Relating to Each Other

Play gives the opportunity for youngsters to build relationships, to plan together, to share, to just talk. Without play they are robbed of building and practicing adequate social skills. When playing together, children decide what they will play, who will go first, and who will play a certain role. What if Sandra is not pleased with the role of mommy that Janet has assigned her? Negotiations take place and both children learn something about getting along with others, perhaps without any adult intervention.

Lack of Persistence and Patience

Children often demand quick and easy gratification. Play gives them the opportunity to develop patience with themselves and others. Play also fosters persistence and productivity on "child terms." Play gives children time to test their ingenuity and capacities. It helps children see what they can accomplish, whether they have built a snow fort, designed a costume, put together a puzzle, built a Lego ship, or acted out a favorite story. These activities take time and develop patience. It is important that these activities offer a challenge the child can meet.

When Jill can work a ten-piece puzzle easily, she can be helped to move onto one with fifteen pieces, not a hundred. Through activities that present a reasonable challenge children begin to experience themselves as growing, learning individuals.

"Be patient toward all that is unsolved in your heart and try to love the questions themselves, like locked rooms and like books that are now written in a very foreign tongue. Do not now seek the answers, which cannot be given you because you would not be able to live them. And the point is, to live everything. Live the questions now. Perhaps you will then gradually, without noticing it, live along some distant day into the answer."[2]

Superficial learning

Many of today's children are highly verbal and can quickly repeat what they hear without fully

---

[2] *Letters to a Young Poet* by Rainer Marie Rilke.

understanding the concept. A young child may know that her birthday is June 5th but have no concept of time and no idea that June is the sixth month of the year.

A young child may count easily to twenty but be unable to bring four napkins when asked. Frequently, children repeat computer terms, but have no understanding of what they mean.

Teachers and parents can be tricked by superficial learners who produce an answer without understanding the process. Adults need to remember that play gives the opportunity to process meaning as the child learns. By playing mommy, by playing school, by putting on a puppet show, children play out their experiences and make sense out of their world. Measuring the milk to make pudding or playing with buttons can give meaning to numbers. Acting out the landing of the Pilgrims or pretending to be Abe Lincoln gives meaning to history. Playing in water gives significance to the ideas of float and sink. Through play young people make sense of their experience.

Hurried Children

Many children are being asked to decide beyond their ability to decide, they are being asked to learn beyond their ability to learn, and they are often overtaxed beyond their energy reserves. Play is an antidote to hurriedness. Tommy, who "did nothing," may be processing the events of a very busy morning in preschool or pondering how to find an acceptable way to join Billy and Chris in their building project.

Lack of motivation

Play encourages children to be initiators, to be organizers of self-directed activities. Youngsters need many opportunities to be planners because they learn from what they initiate. Todd and Greg's haunted house will probably be enjoyed more by its creators than anything adults could have provided for them. Janice is gaining skill in writing letters. The pleasure in this practice is from her desire to work on the mail the way her mother does at work.

Lack of creativity

Play encourages imagination and is at the root of all creativity. It gives opportunities for children to turn boxes into spaceships, paper into hats, and themselves into bears. Play is one of the greatest opportunities that children have to practice using their imagination. Janet, Sandra, Joey, Ben, Janice, Tommy, Billy, Chris, Todd, and Greg are very involved in imaginary play. They are creating their own families, theater, parking garage, and haunted house. Without play there is little time for imagination, thus there is little time for becoming creative.

Play is one of the ways to reduce stress in adults and children without competition or means to an end, just for the sake of doing it. Examples: giving a foot massage, walking the dog, reading a book, and going out to eat.

When teachers and parents create environments where children learn through play, many problems can be eliminated.

CHAPTER 10:
THE DYNAMICS OF DISCIPLINE

Discipline is a Dynamic Process

The word discipline comes from disciple, meaning a leader and a guide. As an adult disciplinarian, your job is to lead and guide your children.

Discipline leads to moral and intellectual development in the child. It focuses on what is being learned rather than on what is happening that moment. For example, when a child spills milk, what do you want the child to learn? To be more careful in the future. Punishment focuses on the consequences and makes the child resentful instead of thoughtful.

Punishment may be effective in the short term, but not in the long term.

There are three outcomes of punishment.

1. Calculated risk. The child will repeat the same act but will try to avoid *being caught*. Many times, the child concludes the price of punishment is worth the pleasure earned.

2. Conformity. When the child conforms, he does not have to make a decision. All he has to do is obey and this assures his security and respectability.

3. Revolt. The child may conform for years, then revolt into constant rebellion and delinquency.

The parent and child struggle and grow as both learn self-discipline. Self-discipline is a complex concept because:

- **It involves how we feel about ourselves.**

- **It involves how we deal with conflict.**

- **It involves how we balance life.**

- **It involves learning limits from our past.**

Who's in Control?

Am I in control or am I being controlled by my child's behavior? Discipline works better if it is done unemotionally. At the same time, parents must also have self-discipline. Adults who beat children and spouses have none.

Behind Bad Behavior

At all ages, some behavior looks like misbehavior, but these show only the force of growth. If you criticize all the time, you are looking for blame, not a solution. React in proportion to behavior. Wisdom is knowing what to overlook, like spilled milk. If you can understand the reasons for your child's behavior, it makes discipline easier.

Be Committed to Your Kid

As a parent, you will encounter a variety of problems that require discipline in your child's growing years. Commitment to your child will help you see beyond the current conflict to the positive qualities you know exist in your child.

I read this story in a newspaper but can't recall the source:

> *A man came from the village every day to buy a newspaper. He could buy from one of two places: the corner stand or the drugstore.*
>
> *The seller on the corner was a real grouch, in a terrible mood all the time. The people in the drugstore were friendly;*

they talked about the news, the beautiful day, etc.

The man would always buy his newspaper from the grouch. His friend observed this over and over in disbelief. Finally, he asked the man why he did that, why he didn't buy from the drugstore. The man replied, "Why should he make a difference in the way I feel?"

The point is this: am I in control of my feelings or is someone else? Discipline is best served without too much emotion such as anger, frustration, or embarrassment. Discipline is best served cool.

Here is another informing story. Many years ago, there was a small primitive tribe on a tropical island that had a special test for sanity. When a citizen of this community appeared to be getting a little looney, he was brough to the main square of the town and put on a platform. There was a running water spigot and underneath was an overflowing bucket; next to it was a ladle.

Citizens would say to the person whose sanity was in question, "Look at all that water. What are you going to do about it? It is running out of the bucket." If the man turned off the spigot to stop the overflow, he was considered sane. But if he began ladling the water out of the bucket without turning off the spigot, it was the looney bin for him. This such a great example of trying to find a simple answer to a complex question.

When we strive to have a nurturing family, a communicating family, one where discipline and rules make sense and are understood, we have to ask why certain things are happening.

Often, we try to find simple answers to complex questions like the person who was just ladling water out of the bucket. The ladling may work for a temporary time, but the problem remains. We need to uncover the real reason behind the behavior. We can either turn the spigot off or understand what the behavior means.

If you understand the reasons for a child's behavior it makes appropriate discipline much easier. We often do not pick up on the clues that our children are giving us. Whenever misbehavior continues, you must deal with the source to eliminate it. Chronic misbehavior is a child's way of telling us something is awry in his life.

At all ages there is some behavior that looks like misbehavior but is really the underlying force of growth.

There is a classic story about an elephant. A group of blind men came across an elephant for the first time. Each touched a different part of the elephant and believed he knew what the elephant looked like. The one who touched the tail said it was a rope. The one who touched the trunk said it was a giant snake. The one who touched the leg said it was a tree, while the one who touched the flank said it was a wall.

Each man experienced the elephant differently and each was sure his answer was correct. None considered there might be another viewpoint. This brings us again to that important word *empathy*. Can you really see the situation from another viewpoint?

We always have to remind ourselves of how it feels to be a child. It is hard to be young and vulnerable. If we can understand this, we can begin to see what discipline really means. The root word of discipline is *disciple*, one who leads and guides our children. Discipline is a teaching process that goes on all the time. A good leader does not use power, force, or harshness. She leads by self-discipline. Understand what the child's behavior means, then go with the positive. Emphasizing mistakes is disastrous.

Eight-year-old Charles was writing a thank you note to his grandmother. His mother asked to see it. Charles reluctantly showed it to her. "Oh,

Charles, look at your horrible writing, it is so messy, you didn't make your lines straight, and you misspelled three words. You can't send that note to grandmother. You'll have to write it over."

Charles labored again, then screamed, "I can't get it right!"

Why can't she look for the positive here? When the mother emphasized the mistakes, she shifted her son's effort from positive to negative. Now he is discouraged and will probably never want to write a thank you note for a long time, if ever.

It would have been a growing situation if mother had mentioned how thoughtful it was of Charles to send a thank you note to his grandmother, found a few well-formed letters, and commented on how nice they looked. Remember we are all parents and children working toward improvement, not perfection. Mark Twain said, "I can live for two months on a good compliment."

Nurturing requires sensitivity to an individual's needs. It isn't what you think they need, or the school thinks, or neighbors think, or society thinks they need, but what that person desires. My daughter, Camilla, wanted her door to be left open, despite the mess. I listened and her open door made a difference.

Nurturing parents help children to see the importance of being human. We related to humanness, not perfection. Do you know any perfect people? Do you like them? We need contact with real people not masked robots. Wearing a mask requires enormous energy, non-productive energy. When we own up to our humanness, we allow others to be human, too.

Florence Cane was an art educator and art therapist. She said, "Since every child is born with the power to create, that power should be released early and developed wisely. It may become the key to joy and wisdom, and possibly to self-realization. Whether or not the child becomes an artist is immaterial." She developed a scribble technique to foster imagination and unconscious imagery.

Here's another example. There were two children. One learned all the names of the trees and could tell you many facts about the wildflowers. The other one climbed trees and walked in the woods. When the two were adults, one decided to bulldoze a forest, pour concrete, and build a store. Which one do you think fought to save the forest?

Some parents tell me they are out of touch with their child by age five or six. There are two aspects of a family: the doing and the being. Both are important. Doing is doing the "dailies," such as shopping, eating, and arguing. Being is knowing what you care about. Being is knowing yourself. Being is knowing me.

What does it take to look at someone in the long view of personhood? It takes time, patience, listening. It takes energy. The better we feel about ourselves, the better we can care for others.

Summary

Closing The Gap
Between What We Know And What We Do

The parent and the teacher each have a crucial role in the development of children. Each instructional role is different:

> **Parents are spontaneous; teachers are more structured.**

> **Parents "bring forth"; teachers "draw out."**

> **Parents and teachers must have confidence in each other.**

> **Parents and teachers together create the map for a child's education.**

> **Each must be a child advocate. The autonomous adult is the result.**

The Educational Map

Key academic skills must meld with key intellectual development in the Educational Map.

Key academic skills:
> Active learning
> Language
> Representation
> Classification
> Seriation
> Number
> Spatial relations
> Time

Key intellectual development:
> Self-esteem
> Climate
> Growth
> Social
> Curiosity
> Play

If parents and teachers close the gap between what we know and what we do, the result will be a successful journey of growth for the child into a mature, autonomous adult, an FFHB.

Remember to strive for parent and child improvement, not perfection.

I often end my classes with this story. Edward Whymper was the first to climb the brutal Matterhorn after six attempts. When he got to the top, he said, "What we want is not to make mountains easier, but people wiser and stronger."

Please evaluate the information in this book by "fitness for use." If it fits, use it; if it doesn't fit, let it go.

APPENDIX I
Learning Contract

In her parenting classes, Carolyn asked her parents to sign this learning contract.

PARENT LEARNING CONTRACT

Carolyn Harden's Basic Class

Before beginning, I would like to propose that you make a learning contract with <u>yourself</u>. The value that you take home from this experience will vary depending on what you bring to this class, as well as the amount of energy you put into it.

My experience with parents has led me to believe that the amount you gain from this class will depend on the "openness" of your attitude and the degree to which you participate in the thinking and the doing.

The purpose of this learning contract is to cause you to stop and think about the kind of commitment you are going to make. It is a contract between <u>you</u> and <u>you</u>. No one is going to see that you sign the contract or attempt to enforce its provisions. You will be the winner for making this commitment.

(1) I will set personal learning goals and work actively to accomplish them. I am responsible for my own learning and will not depend on someone else to "make me grow."

(2) I will be willing to try and practice new skills and experience new behavior.

(3) I understand there are no absolute answers in dealing with human beings and that we are meeting here to understand more about the growth and development of human beings.

(4) I will take what is right for me and "let go" what is not right for me as this is the best way to continue moving forward in my own parenting growth. Each person is unique and what may be right for one may not be right for another.

(5) I will not be too hard on myself, realizing that I need to give my children, as well as myself, the gift of being able to make mistakes, learn, and grow through them.

(6) I will be open about my feelings and reactions so that others may gain from

my insight and have information on which to give me feedback.

(7) I will help others make the most of their learning by providing constructive feedback, and work to promote an environment of trust and acceptance and support.

(8) I will provide honest feedback to Carolyn to help her evaluate and improve her class.

Signature   Date

APPENDIX II

Characteristics of The Carolyn School

These are the requirements Carolyn envisioned for the ideal school:

> Above all, the school is centered on the child, not on the school, curriculum, teachers, staff, or parents.

> The school is developmentally based and focused on prevention of problems rather than detection and correction.

> The child is the end user of the school output, not the parent or the bill payer.

> The school output is a service called education within a visible product, the educated child, accomplished via a process called learning.

> School quality is fitness for use, meaning the end user, the child, determines the quality of the service, either directly or indirectly.

> The educational goal is a Fully Functioning Human Being, FFHB, characterized by autonomy, self-esteem, and maximum development of

their social, emotional, intellectual, creative, spiritual, and physical potential.

The school dynamically meets the needs of its users. As user needs change, school goals and the school itself changes.

Parents are an integral part of the curriculum and the learning process. The uninvolved parents will have less successful children than involved parents.

At startup, there will be a preschool plus a primary unit.

The school has no day care because there is no acceptable substitute for the one-to-one relationship between a caring adult and a child from birth to five years old.

Teachers and staff are partners in the school and share in any financial rewards.
The school's return on investment is intangible, but manifests as competent, contributing human beings.

The curriculum teaches to multiple known learning styles, but not all styles.

The curriculum emphasizes intellectual, creative, emotional, and social needs.

The performance of the school is measurable, albeit incompletely.

School performance quality is evaluated by users, parents, the school itself, and the community.

The staff is evaluated by self and peers, not superiors, against self-developed goals previously approved by the staff that are consistent with school goals.

There is a constant feedback system among users, parents, school, and community.

There is long term follow-up of students after leaving school to continue caring for them and to identify successes and failures of the school.

The school later develops offline profitable products and services to support school goals, such as teacher training services, consultant services, publications, and parenting classes for non-school parents.

APPENDIX III
The Educational Map

The Educational Map:
Programming For Strength
© Carolyn B. Harden

Schools need to close the gap between what is known about child development and what is practiced in the classroom. The educational map provides direction and guidelines to help parents and teachers understand the path children need to travel through their school experiences. The educational map fits the cognitive side with the silent side.

Statement of Need. This need is immediate. More and more children are not ready for kindergarten despite the money, time, energy, and effort in the cognitive side of the curriculum. For success, the cognitive side must fit with the silent side. Together they strengthen the child's autonomy to become an FFHB. Schools need to close the gap between what is known about child development and what is practiced in the classroom. Many teachers, and parents as well, are fooled by superficial learners. These children can quickly repeat what they hear, but do not understand the underlying concepts and processes.

The educational map suggests activities that utilize and exercise all we know about child development in order to counteract student problems like superficial learning and foster successful school experiences.

The goal of the educational map is to provide basic information, in practical "layman" terms, to help parents make wise decisions when working with their children traveling through their school experience. Properly applied, it will decrease the number of children not ready for school, reduce the need for remediation, and improve their emotional health.

The educational map has two parts, the cognitive curriculum and the silent curriculum, and shows how they fit together for the child to develop and increase autonomy and become an FFHB.

The cognitive curriculum includes these key skills: active learning, language, representation, classification and seriation, numbers, spatial relations, and time.

Historically, the cognitive curriculum has received the most emphasis in the educational world when it should represent only about one-fourth of the learning curriculum.

Historically, the silent curriculum has not always been addressed in school. Consequently, many parents are unaware that their child needs to master the silent curriculum as well as the cognitive curriculum to achieve successful living.

The silent curriculum includes the human aspect, self-esteem, the nurturing climate, growth, social development, curiosity, creativity, and play. It should represent about three-fourths of the learning curriculum.

When the cognitive side fits with the silent side, they together make a Fully Functioning Human Being, an FFHB.

In all cases, the curriculum needs to be flexible and allow for individual needs and individual successes.

When parents and teachers can internalize the educational map and apply it to their children and students, a successful journey through the school experience will result in a Fully Functioning Human Being.

Phase 1 of the Educational Map is "Creative Endeavors of the Kid Kind Room." This is a room where children can visit with their parents for a small fee. The room would be staffed with two full-time teachers trained in the Educational Map. The things done in this program need to carry over into the school experience to be helpful in the long term. A book and workbook are planned for parents and teachers to understand and apply the educational map.

Here is Carolyn's proposed general outline of her book, *The Educational Map.*

APPENDIX IV
Speech to the Board
of the Central Presbyterian Church

Taking Action

Carolyn was pro-active on behalf of children and, in a sense, politically active for them. In this case, she wanted to expand the grades in the private school that our daughter, Camilla, attended called Central School for the Young Years. Here is the presentation she gave to the school administration:

Speech to the Board
of the Central Presbyterian Church
Clayton, Missouri
September 27, 1976

Carolyn Harden | Parents' Committee
The Central School for the Young Years

We are here because we are interested in education, community, children, and making the world a better place to live. We are here because we care about Central School. And we would like to see it grow. We are here to consider the question, "Should Central School expand its grades?" We had no guidance from anyone on what to do or how to do it. We went with some of the things we felt were important. We have worked hard and learned a lot. We have read, talked to many people in and out of the field of education, we have talked to children — don't forget them as they have much to offer a listening ear — and we have visited schools. We have facts, statistics, and percentages, which are all important and vital, but without a good product like Central School, there would be no need for this information.

Central School is special, it is unique, and it does have much to offer over other schools. I have talked to many people that visit Central. And they all say there's something so special, so kind, so nice about Central School — something so unique. We would like to help put this uniqueness into words so that all of us can better understand why Central is not "just another school." We have eight reasons.

Number 1. <u>Central works with the total child</u>. Central's philosophy is to work with the physical, social, intellectual, emotional, and spiritual. These are basic needs in developing a total person. Children are created to grow and if we are to help children grow spiritually, as well as intellectually, socially, emotionally, and physically, we must understand clearly the nature of each child at each stage of his development, and how he progresses from stage to stage. It is essential that we know what we can and can't do with him. Without working with every area, only a part of the child will grow, thus resulting in a handicapped person.

Many people are not aware of this concept of the total child and that the process of becoming an adult does roughly follow a pattern. Becoming a full human has no timetable and no rigid limits, but certain stages are apparent, and each one of these depends on having achieved those which precede it.

The child learns to walk before he runs. You must be loved to learn to love. Here is where we rely on the research that has been done on their growth patterns, when they occur, and when and how much a child can do and understand at a given point.

Many times, schools haven't chosen child growth and development principles as their foundation. The child is the most important thing in the school. The child is what the school is all about. Any questions should be answered in terms of WHAT IS BEST FOR THE CHILD, not what is best for anyone else. When in doubt, a school must turn to these principles for the answer. The most important aspect in any school should be the child and his total growth and development, and here there should be no compromise.

Number 2. Central individualizes. The teachers at Central care about each child and consistently go the extra distance to meet individual needs.

Before school begins, the teacher visits with each child in his home. This begins the year with an individualistic approach. Both the child and teacher profit from the visit. The child goes to school knowing he is not a face in the crowd, but a person with a name, someone who has shared, with his teacher, his favorite toy, his room, his home. For the teacher, she gains many insights about the child as she observes him in his home environment. This helps her deal with him as the real person he is.

In the classroom, the teachers strive to find the academic level of the child and go forward from there. Central has done this dealing with many ranges of intelligence, for as you find children, you will find many levels.

An example of an individualizing situation is when one extremely bright child was assigned to prepare information on reptiles—what they eat, where they live, etc. He then reported his information to the class. This was one way of challenging a bright student on one particular morning.

Another example of Central's individualizing is word envelopes. If at any time during the day a child is confused about a word, can't recognize it, doesn't understand the meaning, then they write the word down and put it in the envelope. Later, the teacher can work with the child on those words that are confusing or just interesting to the child.

Central goes even further to individualize with the children. When a child is sick over a period of time, the class will visit, make cards, and make phone calls. One child had an operation and had to begin school late. The child was made to feel a part of his class before he came to school by visits and cards made by the children.

One must recognize that the individualizing process is not easy. It takes much physical and emotional energy. It also takes time, a small teacher-pupil, ratio, and another vital ingredient, dedication. A strong strength at Central is the dedication of the teachers and entire staff.

Number 3. <u>Central helps children learn how to handle their feelings</u>. This area of feeling and communication is an important one which deserves much attention. Children need help in learning why they do something, and also why someone else does something. If a child arrives at school upset at being late because the family overslept, resulting in no breakfast and a harassing mother, the child needs to be able to say, "I'm upset because we overslept, and mother was rushed." After realizing and saying this, the child can go on and salvage the day.

At Central, TIME IS TAKEN TO LISTEN to children and to teach communication skills. If two children have a problem at Central, they discuss and work the problem out themselves. The teachers is there if help is needed. Children have problems, as we all do, and they need practice in learning how to solve the problems themselves. The phrase, "use your words" is often used at Central along with "are you listening to his words?"

Each class has a sign labeled "meeting." If there is a problem, the meeting sign goes up, and all gather to work and discuss solutions. The meeting sign is not only for problems, but also to share pleasant feelings and events.

IALAC appeared on tags worn by the children for many days. It is a lovely way to teach communication, feelings, and understanding another's feelings. IALAC is coming in four days! appeared on the board. The children tried to guess what IALAC meant. They wrote a story about what it was, and some said it was the alphabet, others guessed Fall. IALAC means I Am Loving And Caring. The children and teachers would rub or polish their tags when people would tell or say things to them that made them feel good inside. If someone upset them, they would tear a part of their tag. This may sound rather ridiculous to you, but I challenge you to try it in your family. You will discover that it isn't a silly gimmick just for children. You will discover many things they say, perhaps that cause angry feelings of which you were never aware! Now the children have stopped wearing these tags, but they still polish their hearts, or make a ripping gesture with their hands to help show their feelings.

Central fosters a wholesome self-image for the child, and gives the child opportunities for success, an important ingredient for a healthy self-image. At Central, the self-image is cultivated by dealing with the child as a real person, not as a little adult, using courtesy and respect for the individual in everyday affairs. This seems simple, yet it is surprising how few grownups, including teachers, fail to do so.

Number 4. <u>Central works with problem solving, decision making, learning to reason, and learning how to learn</u>. Central attempts not only to teach adding, but also to have the children use what they learn and learn more about what they have learned. An example of this is the children making crabapple jelly. They use fractions and measuring devices to measure the ingredients for the jelly, to cut the apples in half or fourths, and to read the recipe. This is active learning. The children actually use their five senses needed to do math and reading while they are cooking jelly. It has been proven that children are more likely to remember with active learning.

The world is changing so fast that memorizing facts and spouting out information is no longer enough. In the first grade, 95% of the questions are asked by the children, but by fifth grade, 95% are asked by the teacher. Children should continue to question at all ages and to be guided on how and where to go to find answers to their questions.

At Central, the children did a science experiment. They put a daisy in red colored water. The children were not told what would happen, but were asked, "What do you think will happen?" One child said the daisy would die, another said it would wilt, still others said nothing. Then they waited and watched to see what would happen.

A book of learning games was brought to the classroom. Instead of the teacher reading and deciding which games to choose, the children were given the book during their free choice time. They read it and decided what games they would like to try. The teacher then helped them set up the necessary equipment. They enjoyed the games for many weeks because the children were actively involved in choosing the games.

Questions like "How can we find out?" and "What is your opinion?" stimulate good thinking. These kinds of questions are being asked at Central.

What Central School is really doing is supplying the child with raw materials and good skills so he can develop his own concepts and find out his own answers to God, Jesus, love, friendship, life, and values. With the raw materials of good thinking, he will be able to make wise and intelligent decisions. No one owns the child, or his mind or his body. A wise teacher brings out the child's knowledge, not the teacher's knowledge. Only a wise and human teacher can assess a child's slow and uneven capacity to think and feel and to make wise judgments and choices.

Number 5. <u>Central is teaching the basic skills</u>. This now brings us to the very important basics: reading, writing, and arithmetic. We have discussed communications, feelings, and self-esteem, which are essential because without these you're not likely to have a good learner. But self-esteem alone is not enough. A child must have strong basics skills. Central is unique in that it is delivering both.

Number 6. <u>Discipline</u>. Discipline is always an important question in any school. Central's discipline is free order. It is impossible to individualize a child's learning without some freedom. The child must be free to walk about, and to check out books, magazines, and equipment, but there is no real freedom without some discipline. Central has rules. It has rules that the children know and understand. And many times, the children, with guidance, help to make them. Central encourages freedom with responsibility. Central does not make children raise their hand to go to the bathroom or get a drink of water. They expect the child to be able to handle this responsibility and not play in the water on the way, or stop and visit another classroom, or take an unreasonable amount of time. They give the child the responsibility that he can handle and go from there, adding or subtracting, depending on his level of responsibility.

Number 7. <u>Central show, uses, and lives the Golden Rule</u>. At central, there is compassion for others. A young child wets his pants. This is terribly embarrassing and upsetting to a child. It is handled by saying, "We know up how upset you must be and how bad you feel. I wonder, what we can do to help you feel better? You know this sometimes does happen when we are playing and working so hard that we wait too long." This is compassion in use!

Teachers teach attitudes as well as phonics. Their behavior habits rub off on the children. The teachers' open minds and warm hearts, along with their skills and information, stand out. People stand out in memories and minds more often than facts and words do. People who are loving and help meet a need that a person has are long remembered.

Central children have prayers, Bible stories, and songs. They learn when they are hammering that Joseph was a carpenter and Jesus helped him hammer and saw things. When we work with clay, I mention the this is the way bowls were made in Jesus's time. This is a powerful message to the child. This is the art of using teachable moments to get in a fact, a point, or a message that you want to convey to a child. Teachers at Central are beautifully using teachable moments.

Spiritual growth is being promoted with children at every moment in these everyday experiences at Central. With a walk in the fall, seeing the colors, hearing the crunch of leaves, and smelling the cool fresh air, the teacher can then say, "Oh, what a marvelous job God has done. What lucky people we are to feel so close to Him right here by the leaves." Then go back to the classroom and create a fall experience with painting the fall, writing a fall story, singing a fall song, or pasting a collage of leaves and twigs. The awe and wonder of a fall can bring children very close to God. I would even guess it would bring adults closer, also. How often do we stop and experience the awe and wonder? To love and be filled with joy is to respond to life and the love of God.

At Central, a child wrote on his cardboard lunchbox with magic markers, "I love God." No one told the child to do this. I doubt many even saw it. When I did, it filled my heart with love, just as I'm sure that child's heart was filled with love. This was such a beautiful example of how a child learns about love and God. These events occur daily at Central School. They are what a child stores in his memory bank and takes along in life.

Number 8. <u>Children learn when parents are partners</u>. Central is open and easy for parent participation. The teachers offer an open invitation for parents to observe, or better yet participate, in the classroom. Teachers give parents their home phone numbers at the beginning of the year. They encourage parents to call them anytime the need arises. They are open to parents for conferences at any time in the year. The first and most important influence in a child's life is the home, and Central teachers are aware of its importance in a child's development. The teachers strive to keep communication lines always open between the home and school.

Carolyn's Schooling

Graduated from Barrow School Kindergarten (Athens, Georgia), 1 June 1950 (teachers: Mrs. Howe Chandler and Miss Thelma Elliott).

Barrow School First Grade 1950-1951.

Barrow School Second Grade 1951-1952, (teacher: Miss Thelma Elliott, principal: Mrs. John H. Tarpley).

Barrow School Third Grade 1952-1953, (principal: Mrs. John H. Tarpley).

Barrow School Fourth Grade 1953-1954, (teacher: Gloria M. Hall, principal: Mrs. John H. Tarpley).

Barrow School Fifth Grade 1954-1955, (teacher: M. Day, principal: Mrs. John H. Tarpley.)

Barrow School Sixth Grade 1955-1956, teacher: (Mrs. L. R. Dunson, principal: Mrs. John H. Tarpley).

Barrow School Seventh Grade 1956-1957, (teacher: Mrs. E. C. James, principal: Mrs. John H. Tarpley).

Athens High School, Tennis Team, 1961, 1962. Majorette, 1961-1962, Captain of Military Majorettes, 1962.

University of Georgia, Class of 1965. President of 1962 Pledge Class, Beta Sigma Chapter, of Alpha Chi Omega. Elected to scholastic honor societies: Phi Kappa Phi, 1965; Kappa Delta Epsilon, 1965; Kappa Delta Pi, 1965.

Student Teacher, First Grade, Alps Road Elementary School, Athens, GA, 1965.

University of Missouri—St. Louis student, "Psychology of Exceptional Children," 1984.

Maryville College student, 1985. "Early Childhood Methods: Cognitively Oriented Curriculum," Institute on the Cognitively Oriented Curriculum, Maryville College, June 23-28, 1985.

Gesell Institute of Human Development, taught by Jacqueline Haines.

Carolyn's Employment

1965, summer. Statistician, University of Georgia, College of Education.

1965-66. First Grade Teacher, Childs Street Elementary School, Athens, Clarke County School District, GA, Dorothy Firor, Principal. During the school year the school building was burned to the ground by vandals who entered through Carolyn's locked classroom window in the basement. (From 1909-1915, this building was Athens High School.) $328.75/month.

1966 June 14. Lead Teacher, Project Head Start, Valdosta, GA. State salary plus $100.

1966. First Grade Teacher, Leila Ellis Elementary School, Valdosta, GA. $900.

1966 October 17-June 9. First Grade Teacher, Central Elementary School, Orangevale, CA, San Juan Unified School District, Dale Pingree, Principal. $4,802.00

1967 September 1-June 7, 1968. First Grade Teacher, Central Elementary School, Orangevale, CA, San Juan Unified School District, Dale Pingree, Principal. $6,361.44.

1968-69. Lead Teacher, Project Head Start, Ed Stroud Elementary School, Watkinsville, GA.

1968-69. Remedial Reading Teacher, Oconee County School District, GA. $2,300.

1974-75. Instructor and Kindergarten Teacher, Child Development Center, Florissant Valley Community College, St. Louis, MO. $4,384.50.

1974 September 13. Supervising Teacher, Webster College, Department of Education. $438.45.

1974 December 20. Supervising Teacher, Webster College, Department of Education. $438.45.

1975 February 28. Supervising Teacher, Webster College, Department of Education. $438.45.

1975 March 1. Supervising Teacher, Webster College, Department of Education. $438.45.

1978 November 30. Manchester United Methodist Church Pre-school.

1979 October 4. Carolyn taught "What We Bring to Our Parenting Experience," St. Louis Community College at Florissant Valley.

1980 April 10. Carolyn taught "Self-Esteem: Understanding and Nurturing," St. Louis Community College at Florissant Valley.

1981 October 15. Carolyn taught "Your Child's Self-Esteem" at Ivy Chapel School for Young Children.

1981 October. Carolyn taught "Toy and Game Workshop" at Ivy Chapel School for Young Children.

1982 February 12. Carolyn taught West County YMCA. Pre-School Instructor Workshop.

1982 August 25-26. Carolyn taught Teachers Workshop. Henry School. $85 for six hours.

1984-87. Instructor, Meramec Community College course CCA 102 "Creative Activities for Young Children" $1,194.

Carolyn taught "Enhancing Your Self-Esteem." Parkway East Junior High School Early Childhood Center.

1986-87. Consultant, Kirkwood School District, "Parents as Teachers Program." $250/month.

1986-87. Staff Parent Educator, Kirkwood United Methodist Preschool. $250/month.

1987 April 1-2. Speaker, Kirkwood United Methodist Church Kindergarten Information Night.

1987 April 15. Speaker, Kirkwood United Methodist Church Kindergarten Information Night, "Discipline."

1987 April 22. Speaker, Kirkwood United Methodist Church Kindergarten Information Night, "Siblings."

1987 April 29. Speaker, Kirkwood United Methodist Church Kindergarten Information Night, "Sex."

1987 May 6. Speaker, Kirkwood United Methodist Church Kindergarten Information Night, "Self-Esteem."

1979-1987. Consultant, Parkway School District.

Carolyn was a private consultant, from 1979-1987, teaching classes on child growth, child development, and self-esteem, for 56 different clients on more than 200 separate occasions to over 4,000 people. She also developed special programs for Kirkwood United Methodist Church Preschool and Parkway East Junior High School.

She taught "Parenting: Growth in Self-Esteem for Parent and Child" in six 2-hour sessions over six weeks.

Session 1

This class focuses on the parent, not on the child. I discuss ways people can move forward in their own growth as parents. This class examines what we are bringing to our parenting. What is the real heart of growing as a parent? This class is the foundation for the classes that follow.

Session 2

This class deals with the kind of self-esteem and communication skills we build in our families. All classes have as a basis self-esteem, and how it relates to every area of parenting. To understand self-esteem is to enable us to guide our children and to reaching their own unique potential.

Session 3

This class addresses discipline and behavior. We consider, "What is discipline? What is self-discipline?" We learn how children think, and general guidelines for effective discipline. We also spend time sharing how we handle specific problems.

Session 4

This class deals with play. We think of play as a way of nurturing each part of the total child: social, emotional, physical, intellectual, and spiritual. This class increases our parental awareness of the importance of play. How do children use play as an important developmental tool? As we understand the value of play, we can use it as an important part of our parenting.

Session 5

This class discusses creativity and how we use it to fulfill ourselves. How does creativity help us equip our child for the future? When and how does learning occur?

Session 6

This class visits discipline again. Anger is discussed, and time is spent again considering specific discipline situations.

Carolyn taught "Parenting: Continued Support and Growth in Self-Esteem for Parent and Child" in 10 2-hour classes over 10 weeks.

Carolyn also taught these classes.

Sibling Relationships.
Sibling relationships are important because they influence who a person is becoming while growing up. What can we do as parents to promote positive relationships? How can sibling inter-actions lead to increased self-esteem and self-awareness? How can we moderate children quarrels? Is sibling rivalry always bad?

<u>Sex Education</u>.
Parents bear the primary responsibility for their children's sex education, but rarely have adequate training to do so. This class will consider when and how to discuss sex, and ideas on what to say when we do.

<u>I Can Do It All, Can't I</u>?
This class helps parents understand the basic stages of growth their children go through. As parents understand these stages, they better cope with the characteristics of each age. This is helpful to focus our effort if we as parents can't do it all. We will emphasize the stages of birth to five years, or ages six to ten, or adolescence, depending on the needs of the group.

<u>Play as a Motivator</u>.
Play is a vital and necessary life task. It is one of the most important tools of childhood because it capitalizes on the natural means by which children want to learn. This class will focus on understanding the value of play and how we as parents can become designers, creating a world which allows our children to learn effectively through play.

Exercises that Promote Communication, Self-Esteem, and Understanding.
This class provides an opportunity for parents to learn many exercises to get in touch with their personhood that can be used to enrich the time we spend with our children. These exercises foster sharing ourselves and deepen our relationships with our children. These exercises are fun, easy, and nice to use in a variety of situations.

Creativity and Wonder.
This class teaches parents to look at wonder and creativity as a way to enrich their lives and the lives of their children.

I Know a Lot, Now What?
This class teaches parents how to effectively apply their current knowledge about children to reduce stress and increase energy.

Understanding and Nurturing Self-Esteem.
This class is about the practical under-standing and nurturing of self-esteem in parents and children. What is self-esteem and how can parents help children feel better about themselves?

<u>Self-Esteem: Ours and Theirs</u>.
Living successfully with teenagers requires us to deepen our understanding of self-esteem. This class will emphasize nurturing self-esteem for ourselves as well as our teens.

<u>Become a Child Advocate – the Best Way to Motivate</u>!
There is a crisis in our schools. We need not feel helpless to improve our schools for our children. There are many positive things individual parents can do to help. Some of them must be done together by parents, teachers, business, and the community. We will discuss some options we have his parents to become effective child advocates.

Self-development

In 1977, Carolyn and Jay completed *Parent Effectiveness Training (PET)*, given by Effectiveness Training Associates.

Publications

Author, "Readiness," Childs Street Elementary School, 1966.

Co-author, "Report of the Developmental Philosophy Committee," Parkway School District, 1983.

Author of "Play: Perhaps the Best Teacher You Ever Had" <u>Growing Times</u> magazine (©1985).

Memberships

Association for the Education of the Young Child, 1974-1985.

National Education Association, 1965-1970.

California Teachers Association, 1966-1968.

Georgia Teachers Association, 1965-1966.

Other Activities

Sunday School Teacher, First Methodist Church, Athens, GA.

Vacation Bible School Teacher, First Methodist Church, Athens, GA.

Brownie Scout Troop Leader.

Recognition

Pillar of Parkway Nominee, 1984.

Carolyn's Sources

Ames, Louis Bates. *Your Three-Year-Old.* (one in a series of ages).

Berne, Patricia H. *Building Self-Esteem in Children.*

Bettleheim, Bruno. *The Uses of Enchantment.*

Blume, Judy. *Otherwise Known as Sheila the Great.*

Briggs, Dorothy Corkille. *Your Child's Self-Esteem.*

Cane, Florence. *The Artist in Each of Us.*

Deming, W. Edwards and Mary Walton. *The Deming Management Method.*

Elkind, David. *The Hurried Child.*

Erikson, Erik H. *Childhood and Society.*

Fuller, R. Buckminster. *Critical Path.*

Ginott, Haim G. *Between Parent and Child.*

Hopkins, Emma Curtis. *High Mysticism.*

Lelly, Charles. *The Beautiful Way of Life.*

LeShan, Eda J. *Natural Parenthood.*

McCarthy, Bernice. *The 4Mat System: Teaching to Learning Styles with Right-Left Mode Techniques.*

Miles, Miska. *Annie and the Old One.*

Prather, Hugh. *I Touch the Earth, the Earth Touches Me.*

Prather, Hugh. *Notes to Myself.*

Rilke, Rainer Maria and M.D. Herter Norton. *Letters to a Young Poet.*

Rogers, Carl. *On Becoming a Person.* (and other books)

Satir, Virginia and Barry Ives. *Peoplemaking.*

Snider, Denton Jacques. *The Life of Friedrich Fröebel: Founder of Kindergarten.*

Von Oech, Roger and George Willett, et al.
A Whack on the Side of the Head: How You Can Be More Creative.

In Appreciation

A lot of people over the years helped me bring this work of Carolyn's to the larger world, particularly her colleagues too numerous to mention, but deserved to be, most of whom I have forgotten and some I never met. There are no words of mine to express my profound gratitude to all those advocates for our children. You and the children you teach continue to light this desperate, needing world.

I specifically want to thank Ann E. Schulte, Carolyn's initial editor through October 1987, for her effort with the initial version of this book while Carolyn was fighting the cancer that took her too soon. Ann, wherever you are, I am grateful you kept her book alive long enough for me to pick it up again.

Carolyn's first mentor was Dorothy Firor, the principal of Childs Street School, who hired Carolyn fresh out of the University of Georgia. In my view, she was the greatest influence in Carolyn's professional growth and career.

Mary Ellen Schukai was Director of the Kirkwood United Methodist Preschool when she hired Carolyn as staff educator for Kirkwood United Methodist Preschool, in Kirkwood,

Missouri. That relationship grew in enormous mutual respect and love. When Carolyn died at age 42, I was inconsolable and barely able to function. Mary Ellen, with a group of parents and preschool teachers, commissioned Sue Blackburn Rolston, an artist in Santa Fe, New Mexico, to paint a picture of Carolyn surrounded by children engaged in a variety of her learning activities. It was utilized for the cover art for *Paripassu*, the collection of poems I wrote about Carolyn, published in 2023.

The art also includes a number of her sayings, such as "It takes a lot of slow to grow" and "Life is so daily." The art was painted from numerous long distance phone calls by friends, colleagues, and parents telling Sue about Carolyn and her work. Mary Ellen sold prints to feed the Carolyn B. Harden Memorial Scholarship Fund. I purchased the original art from Sue, framed it, and it now hangs in honor above my bed.

Six months later, 900 copies had been sold and about $7,000, from over 70 contributors, was in the fund. Five preschool scholarships were awarded for 1988-89 from the fund in varying amounts depending on each school's tuition and the family's ability to pay. The money also funded scholarships for 1989-90. I am certain Carolyn would be thrilled to know that her work continued to help children after she left us to wander in another world with a different sense of wonder. I still have a few prints if anyone is interested.

Education scholarships are usually based on high school student performance, but it makes more sense to me, brilliant sense, to award scholarships at the front end of education based on a child's potential to learn, not later and based on what he or she has already learned.

Erika Gerth, Director of Central School for the Young Years, and Dorothea Pflug influenced Carolyn in her professional growth.

There are others, I'm sure, that I cannot recall who deserve credit and appreciation here. I offer my sincere apologies.

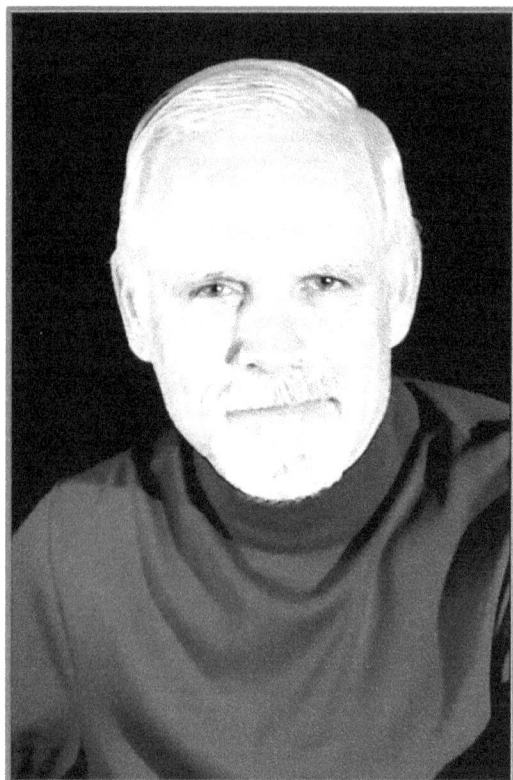

About Jay Harden

Jay Harden grew up in Georgia envying the eagles and hawks, ditching his shoes in summer, and adventuring the alleys, trees, and creeks. Since the beginning, his life has been defined by moments of truth, planned and unplanned.

He survived air combat in Vietnam and navigated his B-52 crew safely home 63 times. After active duty he served in the Missouri Air National Guard and pursued a science career in the Department of Defense, retiring in 1997.

While at the DoD, he helped develop the world's first digital mapping system and co-authored a groundbreaking technical handbook on on cartography that was widely distributed in the Defense Department and beyond. He has since published in numerous anthologies and privately published multiple volumes of family history, poetry, and journals.

He now spends his days writing, painting, photographing, playing guitar, and learning from his five amazing grandchildren.

About Carolyn Harden

*Carolyn was diagnosed with cancer in April of 1987
and left this life on September 22, 1987.*

We met in the fall of 1958 when I was fifteen and she was fourteen. Less than a year later, on May 9, 1959, we planned to be married as soon as one of us graduated from college. This was our secret.

Carolyn was a student in my mother's high school algebra class. She was on the Athens High School girl's tennis team from 1961 to 1962, taught me how to play, and bought me my first racquet.

She was a born teacher; it was her heart's desire. Our high school principal told Carolyn she was not college material and should go to secretarial school, but I convinced her otherwise. She graduated from the University of Georgia in three years and was elected to three scholastic honorary societies. At Georgia, she was also a member of Alpha Chi Omega sorority and president of her pledge class.

The principal apparently did not remember her when he was on the County Board of Education and hired her as a first-grade teacher. She taught first grade at Childs Street Elementary School in

Athens from 1965-1966 and wrote a groundbreaking paper on "Readiness" for the school in 1966. She taught kindergarten, first grade, and remedial reading at different times in Georgia, Massachusetts, California, and Missouri.

Carolyn was a lead teacher for Project Head Start in Georgia in 1966 and again in 1968-1969. She was an instructor and kindergarten teacher at the Child Development Center, of Florissant Community College, St. Louis, from 1974-1975. She also supervised student teachers at Webster College, Webster Groves, Missouri in 1975 and taught at Meramec Community College, St. Louis, Missouri from 1984-1987. Carolyn also found time to be a Brownie Scout Troop Leader from 1976-1978.

From 1979-1987, she was a private educational consultant teaching classes on parenting, child growth, child development and self-esteem, and creative activities for children on over 200 separate occasions to over 4,000 people for 56 different clients.

She also developed special education programs for Kirkwood United Methodist Church Preschool, Parkway East Junior High School, and Ivy Chapel School for Young Children in St. Louis, Missouri. She developed and taught her *Parents as*

Teachers classes to parents in the Kirkwood School District, St. Louis.

Had I to choose one word that described and embodied Carolyn and her life that affected our living together, it would have to be the Greek word *entheos* that means "one out of God." She was wholly and completely alive with *enthusiasm* all her life, one of her many qualities that charmed me into devotion.

Carolyn positively impacted the lives of innumerable children during her teaching career, and I was her witness. I quietly see the effect of her life on our daughter, son, and five grandchildren.

She was an immediate friend to everyone she met and died without an enemy in the world.

She was a gift to the world and the best thing that ever happened to me.

As her husband and editor, I want to leave a song that I wrote for Carolyn in 1999, a song she never heard me sing. (I added the bridge in 2011.)

Wake Me Up, Baby

Wake me up, baby, wake me real slow.
Wake me with loving, tender I know.

Feel my skin, baby, softer than yours,
Due to your touching habit that cures.

Walk with me, baby, tasting the breeze.
Breathe every fragrance, do as you please.

Lay by me, baby, watching the stars.
There are the answers ending all wars.

When I am with you, I'm taking that chance,
Like the moment I met you one Friday night dance.

Your eyes fell upon me, or was it your smile,
That told me we'd marry, at least for a while.

Kiss me once, baby, so it will last,
Stopping the future, ending the past.

Run with me, baby, into the sun.
Together, we gather all we have won.

Yes, we will gather all we have won.

To Contact the Author:
please email
Jay@JayHarden.com

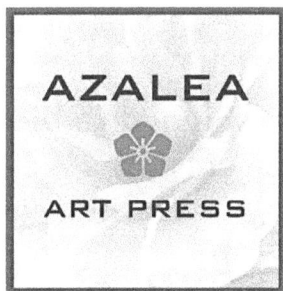

AZALEA

ART PRESS

To Contact the Publisher
please email:
Azalea.Art.Press@gmail.com

For Direct Book Orders
please visit:
Lulu.com

For Signed Copies
please email the Author:
Jay@JayHarden.com

www.ingramcontent.com/pod-product-compliance
Lightning Source LLC
Chambersburg PA
CBHW022019090426
42739CB00006BA/197